# A Lifetime Ago in Baghdad

## An Armenian Family History

# Zagheek Markarian

 FriesenPress

One Printers Way
Altona, MB R0G 0B0
Canada

www.friesenpress.com

The book is composed mainly of stories passed on from generation to generation. This is from our perspective and insight. It is seen and analyzed from our point of view.

ISBN
978-1-03-919364-2 (Hardcover)
978-1-03-919363-5 (Paperback)
978-1-03-919365-9 (eBook)

*1. BIOGRAPHY & AUTOBIOGRAPHY, CULTURAL, ETHNIC & REGIONAL*

Distributed to the trade by The Ingram Book Company

# Introduction

The first of my maternal ancestors left Armenia for Isfahan, Iran, in 1608. Those on my paternal side left Armenia in 1639 and settled in Baghdad, Iraq. I wanted to document different accounts about my family's roots in Baghdad, how life was, and my interpretations and memories. In some interviews or other works, others have referenced my family. Still, they often have inaccurate, distorted, or made-up facts. An example is Sarah Iskenderian's life story and that of my paternal grandfather, Skender Stephan. The different versions of these stories I have heard either come from people meeting me who are part of the Armenian or Iraqi community in Baghdad recounting alleged "memories" or written accounts on the internet, interviews, and even in T.V. series on Iraq Television.

I named the book *A Lifetime Ago in Baghdad: An Armenian Family History* because my life there will never return and now seems surreal; in some instances, stories from that time can feel like they're from tales from *One Thousand and One Nights*: how my ancestors came to settle in Iraq and when I lived there as a child; the ways of life; how the political situation in Iraq impacted their lives and mine; and how we maneuvered to survive. Progress, opportunities, or political change in Iraq will never return those days. Thus, I wanted to document a snapshot of Armenians leaving their homeland and settling in Iraq.

While writing this book, I noticed minimal records available pre-1915 of the Armenian community in Iraq, which could be because they were very private and small. Storytelling was a time I relished in my family. One generation would share the stories with the next. However, over time and due to the nature of word-of-mouth communication, facts become distorted. I wanted to clarify these stories, as I did not wish distorted versions to one day become a reality.

Today, almost four hundred years of identifying as an Armenian Iraqi have ended for us, affecting my children's generation; I wanted to write an account of our journey. Thus, I tried to assemble something for my children, Gabriella and Katia.

My ancestors left Armenia in 1608, and I left Iraq in 1978. The last of my family left Baghdad at the downfall of Saddam Hussain in 2003. Over almost four centuries, we established firm roots in our adoptive country. The old members of my family sharing stories and cultural events make this book possible. I want to thank my parents, John and Edma, Aunt Nimette, and my mother's cousin, Edma Tatossian, for giving me this information. I also would like to thank Winnie Ohanessian, my cousin, for sharing information with me, and Nazar Diran, who seems to be the encyclopedia of identifying faces in Armenian community pictures and also sent me a few photos.

I tried to structure the book entertainingly by sharing truths and anecdotes and through storytelling. I begin by describing what an Armenian is and how our traditions, culture, and the Orthodox Apostolic church influenced our lives. I focus on the first Armenian community pre-1915, who came to settle in Iraq, sometimes detouring. I tried to share and give a feel of life as an Armenian living in Iraq and the people around us. In addition, I shared the story of Sarah Iskenderian as we, her family, know it. I included my grandfather's story, Skender Stephan's, to show how he overcame poverty and lived in Iraq as a successful businessman with innovative business ideas. I also included stories of people with whom we crossed paths. In the final chapter, I wanted to share some renowned family recipes. I plan to add to this book in years to come, but I kept it short to not overwhelm the reader.

Finally, most pictures other than the Adobe and referenced ones belong to the author and are part of a private collection; therefore, they are the author's copyright ©.

Contact: Zagheekmarkarian@hotmail.com.

# Chapter 1

## Armenians

The goal of this first chapter is to offer some introduction to Armenian culture and history to the reader. This includes discussing our religion, the impacts of the history of occupation in Armenia, the genocide against Armenians in Turkey, our loyalty to our fellow Armenians, and more. My objective is not to give a historical account of Armenia nor an explanation of our ethnicity but to write an understanding of how we came to live in Iraq and hold our heritage so closely.

I have always known that we must never forget we are always Armenians, wherever we are, and have come to settle. Our religion and ethnic background are what define us. We are survivors, resilient people, and chameleon-like creatures who have blended in easily wherever destiny took us, but we never lost our identity. We pride ourselves on being Armenians and have honored our legacy, even though we left in the 17<sup>th</sup> century. We seem to have been minorities and immigrants since we left our homeland (Armenia) as far back as 1608, in the case of my ancestry.

We take pride in the fact that we were the first state to adopt Christianity. Most Armenians are Christian Orthodox, and the church headquarters is in Etchimiadzin, Armenia, or Antelias, Lebanon. As Iraqi Armenians, we follow the headquarters in Armenia. Our lives revolve around our church's way of life and feasts. We incorporate attending church and a "feast" with family and other loved ones invited into our lives frequently. The fact that we reside in Muslim countries also makes us hold tighter to our religion and identity.

Armenia has often been under occupation throughout its history. From one time to another, it was under either the Ottomans, the Persians, the Romans, the Byzantines, the Arabs, the Mongols, or the Russians—not until 1918-1920 was the first Republic of Armenia.[1] Our occupiers influenced our cuisine and traditions. Due to the region's agriculture and living conditions, we have similar ways of life and ethnic backgrounds to our occupiers, who are geographically very close to Armenia. However, our religion is pivotal.

A cloud that has scarred every generation since 1915 does reside over us. The trauma of the genocide against the Armenian people in Turkey runs deep, and that feeling of hurt, loss, and

---

1    First Republic of Armenia. (2023, October 1). In Wikipedia. https://en.wikipedia.org/wiki/First_Republic_of_Armenia

anger has been instilled and passed on from one generation to the next. The grief unifies us. The suffering has touched every Armenian family in some way. Besides my paternal grandfather's uncle, none of my family suffered directly in the genocide since they lived in Iraq. Still, they witnessed the Armenian refugees fleeing from the ordeals they faced, sharing horrific stories of genocide just because of their ethnicity. As well as being shocked faced by the ordeals of the refugees, they were threatened with expulsion since Iraq was under Ottoman rule.

As a child, due to communism in the region, Armenia was a place that few could visit. It didn't help that Iraq was becoming a dictatorship, and travel was not as accessible as today. Still, every Armenian hoped to see the homeland of Armenia one day. It became a kind of pilgrimage in an Armenian's lifetime. When you leave your homeland, you hold tightly onto your origin in the new land you settle in, more so sometimes than the people who live back home, who, in time, evolve and modify their lifestyles.

I am very worldly and have met Armenians all over the world. As soon as I mention to another Armenian that I am Armenian, it forges an immediate bond. We must remember we are humans at the end of the day, and there are shortcomings and good and evil in every ethnic group. I am not glorifying Armenians but just pointing out a strong loyalty between us. I would walk two miles to an Armenian business rather than a hundred yards to a non-Armenian one. A force, a magnet, exists that draws you towards your kind. That is probably true for most ethnic groups. However, in our case, many of us have been born and brought up away from our original homeland. In my case, my family has been born outside Armenia for several generations. It is difficult to explain to strangers that although we were born and raised for almost four centuries outside of our homeland, we are proud to be Armenian and strongly identify as Armenians. The reason is that there were no marriages outside our ethnic group, and we kept our religion (Etchimiadzin having a stronghold), culture, traditions, and loyalties towards Armenia.

The influence of our adoptive country is evident in the spoken dialect of the Armenian language and food. The Iraqi Armenian dialect has Arabic, Indian, Turkish, and Farsi words. When Armenians meet each other for the first time, after having established they both are Armenians, the next question is, "So, where are you from?" I would reply, "I am an Armenian Iraqi ."

On meeting non-Armenians and identifying that I am Armenian, often, more so in the past, the following question arises: "Where is Armenia?" You would be surprised how frequently it is assumed we are either part of Russia or Turkey. The answer is simple: Armenians come from Armenia, which borders Georgia, Azerbaijan, Iran, and Turkey. There have been conflicts with the neighboring countries throughout history, causing boundaries to change. Still, we are Armenians living in our state despite foreign invaders ruling Armenia through the centuries. We have our language, alphabet, traditions, and unique culture.

Here are some facts I find interesting about my heritage:

- We are the descendants of Japhet, son of Noah, who built the ark in the Bible. The ark landed on Mount Ararat, now in Turkey.[2]
- In 301 A.D. The Kingdom of Armenia became the first state to adopt Christianity. The Armenian Apostolic Church, to which most Armenians belong, was founded by the apostles Bartholomew and Thaddeus.
- The first church in the world, Holy Etchimiadzin, was built in Armenia in the fourth century. More than 95% of Armenians are Orthodox Christians.
- During christening in the Armenian Orthodox Church, the three most essential sacraments are in one ceremony: baptism, holy communion, and confirmation.
- We initially worshiped fire.
- According to James R. Russell, "The Armenian Cross itself is supported on tongues of flame and has at its center not the body of Christ, but a sunburst." It is a symbol influenced by Armenia's past, evidence of Zoroastrian traditions' spiritual and material culture of Christianity.[3]

---

2    "Hayk." Wikipedia, Wikimedia Foundation, 28 Sept. 2023, en.wikipedia.org/wiki/Hayk. It was accessed on 12 Oct. 2023.

3    §   "Zoroastrianism in Armenia." Wikipedia, Wikimedia Foundation, 26 Sept. 2023, en.wikipedia.org/wiki/Zoroastrianism_in_Armenia. It was accessed on 12 Oct. 2023.

Armenian Cross by Drutska Adobe Stock

- Orthodox Armenians celebrate Christmas and Epiphany on 6 January.
- More Armenians live outside of Armenia than within; approximately 5.6 million (I have seen the figures range between five to ten million depending on where you find the data and how the data is gathered and analyzed) live outside—only 3 million reside in Armenia.
- Armenia's symbols are apricot and pomegranate. These symbols are prominent in Armenian arts, mythology, literature, and cuisine, representing abundance, happiness, marriage, and prosperity.
- I included the Armenian alphabet to show you how unique it is. The Armenian alphabet was developed

around 405 A.D. by Mesorp Mashtots. Initially, it had 36 letters, with two more letters added later.[4]

# Armenian Alphabet

| | | | |
|---|---|---|---|
| ayp | pen | kim | ta |
| yech | za | en | ut |
| toh | zhe | | |

Armenian Alphabet by Drutska from Adobe Stock

- In the Armenian language, there is no differentiation between feminine and masculine. Generally, genders are confused when learning a second language, distinguishing males from females.
- Most Armenians know at least one additional language. Many know more.
- Since leaving Armenia for foreign lands, our church's altar has always faced east towards Armenia. Even when we bury someone, the coffin faces the east, towards Armenia. (East since we seem to have settled on the western side of Armenia, in Baghdad's case, just barely west).

---

4  §  "Armenian Alphabet." Wikipedia, Wikimedia Foundation, 8 Oct. 2023, en.wikipedia.org/wiki/Armenian_alphabet. It was accessed on 12 Oct. 2023.

I tried to keep things simple and not overwhelm the non-Armenian reader with these facts that distinguish Armenians. I grew up with these facts and hoped they would give an insight into who we are.

# Chapter 2

## Earliest Account of Armenian Connection with Mesopotamia

In this chapter, I focus on the first Armenian community in Baghdad in the Medan District in 1639, how they ended up there, and the connections to the Holy Mother of God or Miskinta church.

I searched high and low to find the history of the first Armenians to settle in Baghdad. Due to the region's geography and trade, Armenians could have ventured into Mesopotamia (Iraq) as far back as the Babylonian era.

Indeed, there is a reference to an Armenian from that era that I have always found fascinating because there is a direct link between this Armenian and the place where we ended up. An inscription at Behistun, 539 B.C., about the Persian King Darius the Great referred to an Armenian king. There were many revolts against Persian occupation, the last of which was led by an Armenian, Arakha (Nebuchadnezzar IV). However, King Darius suppressed his revolt.[5]

Many other historical references to Armenians are found in Mesopotamia, mainly due to trade (as previously mentioned). Still, as a community, the first Armenians did not settle in Baghdad until 1639. However, a small community settled in Basra before 1639 due to the city's strategic trade position.

## Kevork Nazarian and Sultan Murad IV

The earliest record I have come across regarding my family is related to Kevork Nazarian, better known as Gog Nazar, who was responsible for the first Armenian community in Baghdad. I am a descendant through my paternal grandfather's side of one of the one hundred families that settled in Baghdad due to him.

The Ottoman (Turkey) Sultan, Murad IV (1612–1640)[6], was known for his political and military successes, and on one of his campaigns in 1635, he recaptured Yerevan, the capital of Armenia, followed by Baghdad, the capital of Iraq, in 1638 from the Safavids. The Safavids were the ruling Persian (Iranian) dynasty at the time. In January 1624, the Persian Shah Abbas I, Abbas the Great, besieged Baghdad. After Shah's death, Sultan Murad IV recaptured Baghdad in 1638, which led to the Treaty

---

5   Lendering, Joana. "Arakha (Nebuchadnezzar IV)." Livius, 2020, https://doi.org/https://www.livius.org/articles/person/arakha-nebuchadnezzar-iv/. Accessed 12 Oct. 2023.

6   "Murad IV." Wikipedia, Wikimedia Foundation, 25 Aug. 2023, en.wikipedia.org/wiki/Murad_IV. Accessed 13 Oct. 2023.

of Zuhab.[7] I do not want to give too many historical accounts in detail since there is an abundance of literature that the reader can look into that would provide detailed, in-depth reports of historical events at this time that do a better job than I could ever do.

Sultan Murad IV's victory in Baghdad was due to the contribution of Kevork Nazarian, an artillery officer who built an instrumental cannon in 1638. The cannon hit one of the gates of Baghdad, Bab-Al Madham. Unfortunately, Allied forces destroyed this gate when they captured Baghdad during World War I, erasing the physical history of this contribution.

Bab Al-Madham was part of Iraq's heritage and significant to its defenses over the centuries. Abbasid[8] Abu Ja'far al-Mansur built Baghdad in a circle during the mid-700s A.D. with four gates to protect it from foreign invasions. The gates are Bab Al-Madham, Bab Al-Sharqi, Bab Al-Taisim, and Bab Al-Wastani.

---

7    "Treaty of Zuhab." Wikipedia, Wikimedia Foundation, 3 Oct. 2023, en.wikipedia.org/wiki/Treaty_of_Zuhab. Accessed 13 Oct. 2023.

8    Chambers, Richard L. "The Abbasid Caliphate." Britannica, 23 Jan. 2023, www.britannica.com/place/Iraq/The-Abbasid-Caliphate. Accessed 13 Oct. 2023.

Bab Al Sharqi in 1930 by Aresen Hovakimian

Bab Al Sharqi in 1930 by Arsen Hovakimian

Canon Tob El Kheramah June 1930 by Arsen Hovakimian

Bab-Al Madham in 1930 by Arsen Hovakimian

Holy Mother of God or Miskinta by N. Diran

Sultan Murad was so happy with his December 25, 1638 victory that he wanted to reward Kevork. He asked Kevork what he wanted, and Kevork asked for a church for the Armenians and permission for one hundred families to settle in Baghdad. He received his gift in 1639, the Church of Sourp Asdvadzadzin[9], better known as Holy Mother of God or Miskinta, built in the Medan district. The church used to belong to the Assyrians. As previously stated, the altar in Armenian churches always faces east towards Etchimiadzin (the Armenian religious headquarters in Yerevan). In this church, it doesn't. Then, the Armenian community in Baghdad was born, establishing roots.

The Armenians built on the church, especially over the years. Kevork Nazarian brought relics of the forty martyrs of

---

9    "The Church Sourp Asdvadzazin in Baghdad (Church of the Holy Mother of God, "Miskinta")." Mesopotama Heritage, 1 Jul. 2017, www.mesopotamiaheritage.org/en/monuments/leglise-sourp-asdwadzadzin-de-bagdad-eglise-de-la-sainte-mere-de-dieu-dite-miskinta/. Accessed 10 Oct. 2021.

Sebaste from the 12th Roman Legion who came from different towns and villages in Armenia. The story of the martyrs occurred near Melitene in Turkey. Under orders, the commanding officer told forty soldiers they would be placed in a freezing lake to die unless they renounced their faith. One did so and died instantly; the others didn't. The following day, halos appeared, crowning their living heads. It impacted one guard who witnessed this; at that point, he proclaimed himself a Christian and joined the remaining thirty-nine, making them forty again. Lucias, Duke of Caesarea, ordered their execution, making them martyrs. These forty martyrs are the soldiers in history known as "Karasoon Mangoonk" (Forty Children). In the twentieth century, relics were found within the walls when the church was under construction. I am unsure of the significance of moving those relics to the Holy Mother of God or Miskinta church, but it shows that the community has established firm roots.

Medan District 1930 by Arsen Hovakimian

Medan District 1930 by Arsen Hovakimian

Medan District 1930 by Arsen Hovakimian

As a child, the church was significant to my family, especially since my father's family was from the Medan district. People went there to make vows despite not being Armenian Christians. Pilgrimages also took place. I remember at the church, there was a chain with a large clasp; a person who made the vow would put the chain around their neck, and if it opened, God would accept the vow. Donations marked every celebration or occasion, whether religious or for a life event; gratitude usually took the form of slaughtered sheep, money distributed amongst the poor, or gifts for the church's needs. It was a church we went to for hope and thanks. At the Feast of Our Lady, a yearly feast held at the church, I remember that the church would be so crowded that you couldn't get in; even Muslims would attend. We often forget that both religions believe in the same God and that there are several mentions of the Virgin Mary in the Quran.

Holy Mother of God or Miskinta Alter by N. Diran

Antaran Tatossian and Kerob Sethian 1895

The church has three graves; one, we know for sure, is related to my family's history. That is the grave of Antaran Tatossian, who died in childbirth. Her father was so distraught that he decided to keep her close and buried her there. Antaran is the sister of Mariam, my mother's paternal grandmother, and the sister of Madool, Regina's mother (Regina established the Old People's Home in Baghdad). Antaran was the daughter of Ovaness and Shushan Tatossian (who bought Annana). At the same time, Antaran was the sister of my mother's maternal great-grandmother, Eliza; good luck sorting out the connections in your head. Whenever we entered the church, my mother used to warn me to be careful and not step over her grave as it is at the entrance, and I should respect her. I believe the church has paved over the graves.

There is a picture of Antaran and her husband. After her death, her husband (Kerob Sethian) remarried Mariam Der Yeghiaian from my father's side, an aunt of my grandfather Skender on his maternal side. After their marriage, they moved to France.

Antaran's husband, Kerob Sethian, with his new family (married to Mariam Der Yeghiaian), moved to France in 1912.

I found another picture of Antaran sitting with her sisters, Eliza and Madool, and her niece, my great-grandmother Zagheek.

Top: In the middle of the second row, Zagheek Ohanessian is standing. From right to left, second Antaran, next to her Madool, and next to her Eliza (née Tatossian). 1897

The Church of Sourp Asdvadzadzin served the Armenian community for over a century. Between 1847 and 1864, Supreme Vartabed Mesrob arrived from Istanbul and coordinated efforts to raise the necessary funds to build a bigger church, even getting contributions from Istanbul from wealthy Armenians while obtaining the edict from Constantinople. He also brought the Sourp Yerrortutiun (Holy Trinity) altar painting that was supposed to be for a church in Istanbul. All Armenians contributed—even people experiencing poverty offered their wedding bands. He went door to door, collecting whatever he could. He exceeded his target, even using surplus donations to build another church in the north. In 1850, the construction of the church began.

Mesrob was also responsible for assembling accurate records of the Armenian community. The Armenian Baghdad diocese was previously attached to New Julfa in Isfahan; this was detached in 1848 and fell under the direct responsibility of the patriarch of Istanbul. That has been one of the major obstacles I faced with my ancestors' records. It is only due to Mesorb's efforts to keep them in Iraq after the 1860s that records of my family exist in Iraq, but before that, it has been challenging to access the old records. On 21 December 1852, in the Shorja quarter, the Church of the Holy Trinity opened its doors. The Armenian prelacy building was situated somewhere inside the yard of the Holy Trinity Church.

The Church of the Holy Trinity in the Shorja quarter always had foundation issues. Groundwater flooding constantly occurred, damaging the church. At the time, there wasn't the technology available to us now to remedy this problem. Several of my ancestors' graves were there, with Minas Minas, one of the last congregation members, buried there. However, when his wife Eliza died, she had requested to be beside her deceased husband, and the foundation was flooded and drained. The congregation tried to fix the issue several times and gathered donations, but their attempts failed. Finally, the Armenian Church Committee decided shops would be built on the land, establishing "Souk Al Armen," or the Armenian market. I understand the Church does not exist, although a plaque is there to commemorate it.

Later, "St. Gregory, the Illuminator," another church, was constructed to hold 1,000 people, indicating how the Armenian community had grown. When the Armenian community was at its peak, three parallel lines of parked cars against the pavement would block the traffic around the church at feasts. The church burst at the helms, with people overflowing into the courtyard and the cemetery.

In 1903, the construction of the Armenian cemetery in Baghdad took place, and that is where my ancestors started to bury their loved ones. Before the Holy Trinity Church, the previous cemetery was at Athamia and was closed due to the iron bridge (Jeser al Hadeed). A few decades ago, the graveyard of 1903 became crowded, forcing the community to use a new cemetery designated in its place for burials outside Baghdad.

Sadly, the Armenian congregation has depreciated in Iraq considerably since 2003. It is sad since we helped build the land, helped it flourish, called it home, and have so much affection towards it, the land we settled in four centuries ago, and now we are strangers to it. Sharing our history is essential, and it is part of our DNA. We were a small community when we settled, but now we have become a small community again. I don't want our efforts and love for Baghdad, a place we called home for centuries, for us to be airbrushed away in history.

# Chapter 3

## The Persian Connection and the Thaddeus Family

My research shows that most Iraqi Armenians are related to each other differently since they married within their small community. The same people are connected many folds over. I know this through church records and my family tree. However, distinguishing how someone can be an aunt from one side of the family and a cousin at the same time from another part of the family can cause your head to explode. I asked my mother about the family's most complex and interwoven relationship. She shared that it is between my uncle (her brother) and his children. Araxi is the maternal grandmother to my cousins (his children) and the first cousin to my uncle, making their mother their second cousin, and this is only considering the close relationships. My cousins can be third and second cousins to their grandmother simultaneously. That is even overlooking other relationships since there are many different connections. The distinct background of Iraqi Armenians also adds to how uniquely we are interrelated. The pre-1915 community in Baghdad had settlements from Armenia and, in my case, also Armenians who made a detour and settled in Isfahan and India (Bombay and Calcutta) and ended up in Iraq because of either their British ties or already having relatives in Baghdad.

Close-up portrait of Shah Abbas the Great with an Arabian-style rich turban on the head. Ancient grey tone etching style art by Lebovis, Magasin Pittoresque, 1838 By Mannaggia Adobe Stock

In 1608, Shah Abbas of Persia, from the Safavid dynasty, was at war with Russia. His army advanced to Russia through the Caucasus via Armenia. While in Armenia, he observed the people and their way of life. He admired the Armenian people's ingenuity, whether in business or craftsmanship. The Safavids ruled eastern Armenia while western Armenia remained under Ottoman rule. Abbas I of Persia adopted a strict policy in the region to his north-western boundaries against the Ottomans; this involved the compulsory resettlement of Armenians. Shah Abbas relocated around ten thousand families from Arax Valley (now in Azerbaijan territory) to Isfahan (Persia), called New Julfa, named after the older Julfa in Nakhiavan.[10]

Iran Political Map By Peter Hermes Furian Adobe Stock

10    "Iranian Armenia (1502–1828)." Wikipedia, Wikimedia Foundation, 10 Oct. 2023, en.wikipedia. org/wiki/Iranian_Armenia_(1502%E2%80%931828). It was accessed on 13 Oct. 2023.

At this time, Armenians led a peaceful life with liberties. They built churches and schools and enjoyed religious, cultural, and traditional freedoms; they were happy in the life they led, which was made possible by Shah Abbas. Some of my family members were the artisans of the mosques built in Isfahan. Isfahan was south of Tehran and the capital of Persia at the time.[11] I hope to visit those mosques and admire those masterpieces one day.

Shah Abbas's expectations of the Armenians' dexterity in commerce paid off. The community became active in cultural and economic development, especially in the silk trade monopoly, which they controlled. Armenians were very active in trade, threatening the English and the Dutch traders, venturing into opportunities neglected by these parties, and eventually pushing the Dutch out. They utilized the ports and stationed each other strategically, so Armenians managed the whole trade route. Five families monopolized trade, but the most prominent was Khoja Minas of Surat (he had extensive trade activities in Surat). He even ventured out to the Philippines. At first, his relationship with the English was amiable, but his rise and trade domination made them enemies, leading to his bankruptcy. His successors decided to work with the British through the East India Company and serve in the British Residency. My mother shared that the Minas's house in New

---

11  "The Role and Reason Why Armenians Were Selected As Iranian Businessmen During the Shah Abbas's Era." International Journal of Scientific Research and Management (IJSRM), vol. 7, no. 11, Nov. 2019, pp. 579-84, https://doi.org/10.18535/ijsrm/v7i11.sh03.

Julfa is still there; my mother's cousin visited it on her visit to Iran in the 1950s.

Shah Abbas the Great died in 1629, and things started to change. In 1694, Shah Husayn[12], the last of the Safavids dynasty, ascended to the throne. Shah Husayn handed state affairs to a Muslim cleric who enforced Sharia law. Islam heavily influenced Sharia law and discriminated against the Christian Armenians. Even illegally taxing the Armenian churches heavily at one stage.

Meanwhile, Sultan Husayn indulged in alcohol and the pleasures of his harem. Armenian liberties were slowly disappearing. His successors were not any better. Finally, my ancestors decided it was better to immigrate again. Some went to Baghdad, some to India, and some to Basra. An elderly Armenian gentleman once told me, "As soon as we left our homeland (Armenia), we became immigrants. When we eventually returned to Armenia, we were foreigners." As much as we contribute positively, we are never genuinely accepted in that region.

---

12 "Soltan Hoseyn." Wikipedia, Wikimedia Foundation, 11 Sept. 2023, en.wikipedia.org/wiki/Soltan_Hoseyn. Accessed 13 Oct. 2023.

# Thaddeus Family Tree

Based on Information from David J. Thaddeus

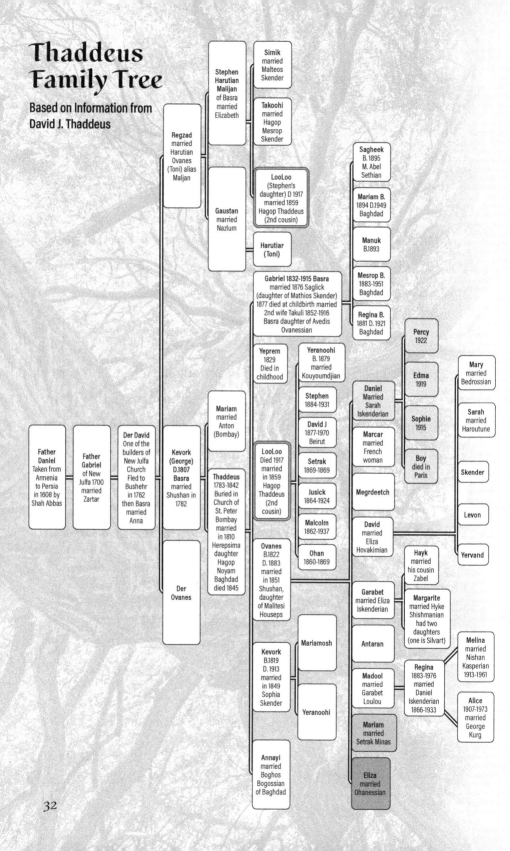

Father Daniel Taken from Armenia to Persia in 1608 by Shah Abbas

Father Gabriel of New Julfa 1700 married Zartar

Der David One of the builders of New Julfa Church Fled to Bushehr in 1762 then Basra married Anna

Kevork (George) D.1807 Basra married Shushan in 1782

Der Ovanes

Mariam married Anton (Bombay)

Thaddeus 1783-1842 Buried in Church of St. Peter Bombay married in 1810 Herepsima daughter Hagop Noyam Baghdad died 1845

Regzad married Harutian Ovanes (Toni) alias Maljan

Stephen Harutian Malijan of Basra married Elizabeth

Gaustan married Nazlum

Simik married Malteos Skender

Takoohi married Hagop Mesrop Skender

LooLoo (Stephen's daughter) D 1917 married 1859 Hagop Thaddeus (2nd cousin)

Harutiar (Toni)

Gabriel 1832-1915 Basra married 1876 Saglick (daughter of Mathios Skender) 1877 died at childbirth married 2nd wife Takuli 1852-1916 Basra daughter of Avedis Ovanessian

Sagheek B. 1895 M. Abel Sethian

Mariam B. 1894 D.1949 Baghdad

Manuk B.1893

Mesrop B. 1883-1951 Baghdad

Regina B. 1881 D. 1921 Baghdad

Yeprem 1829 Died in childhood

Yeranoohi B. 1879 married Kouyoumdjian

Stephen 1884-1931

David J 1877-1970 Beirut

Setrak 1869-1869

Jusick 1864-1924

Malcolm 1862-1937

Ohan 1860-1869

LooLoo Died 1917 married in 1859 Hagop Thaddeus (2nd cousin)

Ovanes B.1822 D. 1883 married in 1851 Shushan, daughter of Malitesi Houseps

Kevork B.1819 D. 1913 married in 1849 Sophia Skender

Annayi married Boghos Bogossian of Baghdad

Mariamosh

Yeranoohi

Daniel Married Sarah Iskenderian

Marcar married French woman

Megrdeetch

David married Eliza Hovakimian

Garabet married Eliza Iskenderian

Antaran

Madool married Garabet Loulou

Mariam married Setrak Minas

Eliza married Ohanessian

Percy 1922

Edma 1919

Sophie 1915

Boy died in Paris

Hayk married his cousin Zabel

Margarite married Hyke Shishmanian had two daughters (one is Silvart)

Regina 1883-1976 married Daniel Iskenderian 1866-1933

Mary married Bedrossian

Sarah married Haroutune

Skender

Levon

Yervand

Melina married Nishan Kasperian 1913-1961

Alice 1907-1973 married George Kurg

The Thaddeuses stream is interwind with the Minas stream. According to David J. Thaddeus, this is how they came to live in Baghdad after leaving Persia, with detours, again due to opportunities and circumstances, to better the quality of their lives. This account can be confusing and wordy, but I wanted to include all the names as a record source since no references exist. The head of the Thaddeus family goes as far back as 1700 to New Julfa, the first to settle there. He was a priest named Gabriel, an official of the clergy. Father David, his son, succeeded him, whose name appears as one of the church's builders in New Julfa; due to the oppression and tyranny in Persia in 1762, since Shah Abbas I's reign, things declined considerably with each successor. He, his wife Anna, his two sons, Father Ovanes and Kevork (George), a minor, and his only daughter Regzad fled to Bushehr and Basra.

Kevork became a successful trader. Many Armenians excel in business and craftsmanship, a trait aided by the fact that they, as stated earlier, are often fluent in two or more languages. Kevork was no exception due to his linguistic ability; he worked for the East India Company in Basra. The East India Company once controlled a substantial percentage of world trade. The family decided to buy shares and serve in the company. There is an account that he once was responsible for capturing two French spies who were on their way to India for the sake of rebellious action in the time of Napoleon Bonaparte in what is now known as Kuwait. Due to his efforts in this instance, he was rendered a valuable serviceman to the British.

Kevork married Shushan in 1782 and had a son named Thaddeus in 1783 and a daughter named Mariam. Mariam married an Armenian called Anton; they moved to Bombay and had two sons, Golustan and Stephan. Our ancestors in Bombay, including Anton, set up a trust to sponsor a mass for the deceased once a year in Baghdad, but in 1947, when India achieved its independence, this stopped due to obstacles for money transfers. We did not know the trust existed. The Armenian Orthodox Church diocese in India references my mother's family, primarily through their contributions.

In 1807, Kevork died in Basra, and Thaddeus carried on with his father's trading business and other interests in India. He also served in the same capacity as his father as an interpreter for the British Political Agency (British Residency) in Basra. In 1810, he married Heipsina. They had a daughter, Annayi, who married Boghos and moved to Baghdad, and two sons, Ovanes and Kevork. Sadly, as a businessman, Thaddeus failed, and he decided to return to Bombay to collect from his business associates, salvage something, and educate his sons. He moved in with his sister Mariam. Thaddeus died in 1842. His grave is at Bombay's Armenian Church of St. Peter at the courtyard entrance.

In 1844, Sir Henry Creswicke Rawlinson, 1st Baronet, was a British East India Company army officer. While in Bombay and on his way to Baghdad, he realized there was poor clerical support for the British Residency in Baghdad, and he advertised in the *Bombay Times* for two clerks. Kevork and Ovanes got the positions and moved to Baghdad. Finally, they could relocate and be close to Annayi. It took their families three months to follow them, and on 31 March 1845, the families were reunited and started to settle. Kevork oversaw the accounts, and Ovanes was one of the secretaries. In the community, they were referred to as "Bait al Ketab," meaning the "house of writers," due to their profession in the British Residency. Hagop and Gabriel, Kevork's sons, were later employed in the residency. Hagop was a translator, and Gabriel was a treasurer. Due to their long terms with the British Residency, which spanned two generations, they were awarded British nationality, among other family members. Some family members traded on behalf of the East India Company, looking after British interests. British nationality was granted to them, enabling them to be more mobile in the region. Future generations will strengthen their ties by living in the U.K. or being born there. As fate will have, it is where I ended up and grew up. It is a nationality we value and are grateful for. It gave us dignity and protected us in the Middle East.

British Residency in Baghdad June 24, 1930, by Arsen Hovakimian

In fact, at that time, the British Residency paid very little, but the employees could subsidize the low pay by getting commissions through different cases they managed. Ovanes was assigned one such "case" that changed his fortune more than he had imagined. At that time, the successors of such dynasties in Persia (Iran) or Turkey killed immediate successors to the throne who could threaten their position to ensure they stayed in power. In Persia, one of Shah's wives ran away from Persia to Iraq, fearing her son's safety (Abbas Mirza II) upon Mohammad Shah Qajar's death and the succession of his oldest son and half-brother to Abbas Mirza II, Naser al-Din Shah Qajar, whose mother, Malek Jahan Khanom, was an influential and fearful figure. The mother of Abbas Mirza II requested protection for herself and her son from the British Residency on arrival in Iraq. They designated Ovanes Tatossian as her liaison de affairs. He served her with dedication and loyalty.

Sadly, Abbas Mirza II passed away in infancy. Ovanes considered the Shah's wife's safety more than his family's because of her delicate position. She made a deal with Ovanes; he would look after her and be responsible until her death. In return, he would inherit her wealth. Her wealth was legendary. My mother's great-grandmother, Eliza, talked about the jewels handed to them on visiting her as children, the bowls filled with gemstones. After a few years, Abbas Mirza II's mother also passed away. As a result of his inheritance, Ovanes bought Annana. Annana is an estate (Ameeriya) comprising farming parcels close to Hillah. The land covered from Hindiya Barracks to the end of Babil near Hillah. There are wetlands with rice and orchards that grow different kinds of fruit. It is situated on the Euphrates River and is used to irrigate these farms. The area we owned covered half an hour by car from one end to the next. The guards planted date trees along the route (more stories on our guards, especially one named Adai, come later). When my mother and her siblings were young, they often went to Annana and crossed the river by "Guffa," a circular boat, to visit the Lions of Babylon. They stayed at the palace built there.

Later, in the 1960s, Arab farmers, employed by my family or leasing land from them, decided to build on it and said they would kill the owners, my ancestors, if they set foot on the vast property since they were British. The farmers owned a third of the land, another third by the government, and the final third by my ancestors. On the acres of land, there were villages. It was a time of political change in Iraq. Like Muasker al Rasheed, Abdul Kareem Qassim, Prime Minister of Iraq in 1958, nationalized the area with little compensation, never claimed by the owners. Someone mentioned that Saddam Hussain built a magnificent palace there when he was in power. I am not sure what happened to the palace built by my ancestors. I still have the deed to those lands, proving we are the rightful owners. Looking at the state of Iraq and the corruption that has engulfed it, I am not holding my breath to get our lawful legacy back. I witnessed firsthand the corruption, which broke my heart since it was a country with so much potential and strong ethics.

Iraq's political map includes the capital, Baghdad, national borders, important cities, rivers, and lakes. Called Mesopotamia, the land between Tigris and Euphrates. English labeling. Illustration. See Less By Peter Hermes Furian Adobe Stock

Annana 1928

Annana, bought for agricultural purposes, is close to Hillah and Hindiya Barracks, on the other side of the Euphrates River, across from the famous Lions of Babylon, a historical theme in the region, considered essential symbols of Babylon in particular and Mesopotamian (Iraq). As well as serving as a farming area, my family often went there for picnics or to get away. I found some pictures taken in the 1930s. In one image, during a visit to Annana, my family took the boat and crossed over to the other side. The photograph shows them in front of the lions. Incredibly, those historical artifacts have survived through the centuries, enduring harsh weather conditions.

Annana 1928

Annana, crossing to the Lions of Babylon 1928

From Annana, they would travel across the Euphrates
River to get to the Lions of Babylon. 1931

Immigrating is not easy. It is starting new, leaving what you know, and starting from the beginning. Taking such a risky step is something I admire and respect. At the time of my ancestors, I could not imagine immigrating since the distance and time required were significant, and coming back should things not work out is difficult. Yet they were brave enough to take the challenge to better their lives with a better income, liberties, and freedoms. They left their homeland in Armenia, went to Persia, detoured to India, ended up in Iraq, and yet again left for different corners of the world.

# Chapter 4

## Minas Family

The Thaddeus and Minas streams intertwine, but Minas's stream is directly my mother's, Edma, through her father, Vartan. In this chapter, I focused on different members of the Minas family, their direct British connection, and the strained relationships that now exist.

# Minas Family Tree

* Some of the dates of the new generation are guesses

Ana Khatoon — Agha Minas

Agha Khacheeq Megrdeech 1800-1858

Mariam Khatoon

Agha Mukail 1808-1882

Tang Khatoon

Ossana married in 1859 Steven Lynch D. 1864

Setrak 1845-1894

Misak

Sophie 1856-1895 married Ohanes Iskenderian 1834-1899

Serpuhi a.k.a. (Umm Melkon)

Eliza a.k.a. Mukastan

Mariam Tatossian

Khachik

Minas 1880-1947 married Eliza Iskenerian

Zabel 1891-1897

Sara 1889-1960 married Daniel 1875-1922

Krykor 1886-1887

Percy 1922

Edma 1919

Sophie 1915

Boy died in Paris 1913

Vartan 1894-1944 married Arsina Hovakimian 1905-1983 (cousin)

Arousiak (Aroos) 1885-1948 married Markar Hovakimian

Zabel 1890-1960 married Hyke Tatossian (Cousin) 1883

Araxi 1917-2005 married Abcar Ohanessian 1907-1975

Zagheek 1912-2003 married Malcolm Cambel

Lala 1928-1984 married Arshak

Mary 1921-1963

Nimette 1939 married Louis Apikian 1937-2020

Edma 1938 married John Stephan 1937

Edmond 1935-1994

Amira 1948-2016

Winnie 1954 married Aris Kassibian 1948

Ohan 1956 married Anita Tajirian

Basil 1958-1985

Rudy 1960 married 1st Reem Sarafa 2nd. Maral Kishmishian

Tania 1967 married Georges Ghanem 1965

Liyon 1977 married Rana

Tara 1976 married Edmon Tajirian

Vahe 1972 married Nour

Vartan 1967 married Ghada

Taleen 1991

Anne 1988

Abcar 1986

Dina 1984 married Sevag Demirjian

Nairi 2006

Naro 2004

Basil 2003

Lala (Mother Reem) 1996

Katia 1995

Gabriella 1993

Margaret 2000

Vaughn 1997

Minas 2001

Arsina 1997

Maral 1982 married Tamam Khadduri 1981

Dhana 1981 married Bassam Khadori 1980

Andrew

Christina 2012

Maria 2010

Edmond 2006

Nayira 2019

Aria 2017

Rose 2017

David 2018

Ruben 2016

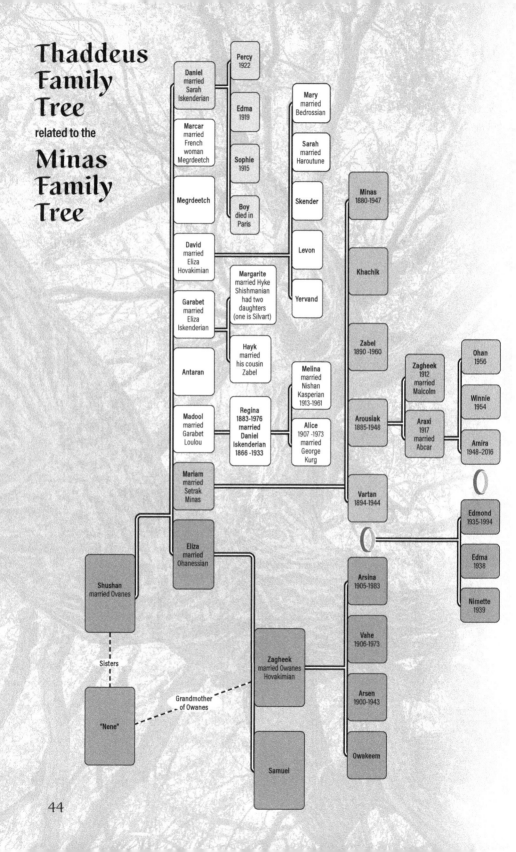

# Thaddeus Family Tree

### related to the

# Minas Family Tree

**Daniel** married Sarah Iskenderian

**Percy** 1922

**Edma** 1919

**Sophie** 1915

**Boy** died in Paris

**Marcar** married French woman Megrdeetch

**Megrdeetch**

**David** married Eliza Hovakimian

**Mary** married Bedrossian

**Sarah** married Haroutune

**Skender**

**Levon**

**Yervand**

**Margarite** married Hyke Shishmanian had two daughters (one is Silvart)

**Garabet** married Eliza Iskenderian

**Hayk** married his cousin Zabel

**Antaran**

**Madool** married Garabet Loulou

**Regina** 1883-1976 **married** Daniel Iskenderian 1866 -1933

**Melina** married Nishan Kasperian 1913-1961

**Alice** 1907 -1973 married George Kurg

**Mariam** married Setrak Minas

**Eliza** married Ohanessian

**Minas** 1880-1947

**Khachik**

**Zabel** 1890 -1960

**Arousiak** 1885-1948

**Zagheek** 1912 married Malcolm

**Araxi** 1917 married Abcar

**Ohan** 1956

**Winnie** 1954

**Amira** 1948–2016

**Vartan** 1894-1944

**Edmond** 1935-1994

**Edma** 1938

**Nimette** 1939

**Shushan** married Ovanes

Sisters

**"Nene"**

Grandmother of Owanes

**Zagheek** married Owanes Hovakimian

**Samuel**

**Arsina** 1905-1983

**Vahe** 1906-1973

**Arsen** 1900-1943

**Owakeem**

44

Agha Minas in his old age          A painting of Agha Minas

The churches in Calcutta and Bombay have records of our ancestors there. They also served in the East India Company after leaving Isfahan. Unfortunately, in 1874, the East India Company was dissolved. The family decided to sell their shares well before it disbanded, allowing them to receive a large percentage of the revenue through dividends and profits on their investments. They did so since they had decided to leave and join their relatives in Baghdad.

Agha Minas is the patriarch of the family. He is my great-great-great-grandfather. He established firm roots in Baghdad through the profits he had made, along with his son, Agha Mukail, his daughter, Mariam Khatoon, and another son (who died young) and mother, Ana Khatoon; they bought land, including Garara (Masbah), a seven-million-square-meter estate. They later divided it into seven parcels of land, and each lot was one million square meters, but over time and with the expansion of the family, the descendants began to sell off the shares.

Agha Mukail

Agha Mukail's son Setrak

The Ottoman Empire besotted "Agha," a form of honorific title, upon Agha Minas, his son, Agha Mukail, and Agha Khatcheeq (Agha Mukail's father-in-law), the father of Tang Khatoon, the wife of Agha Mukail. The title "Agha" is like "Lord." This title is for any male who is influential or respected. The title "Agha" is not given to women, but "Khatoon" is added to their name as a form of respect, like Tang Khatoon and her husband's grandmother, Ana Khatoon. Ana Khatoon was a modern woman who enjoyed riding horses with the British

Ambassador's wife and was a firm fixture in Armenian society. The title of "Agha" is not inherited.

Unfortunately, when my Aunt Nimette's home got looted after the fall of Saddam in 2003, the looters destroyed everything, even the honorary decree that granted my ancestors the title of "Agha." She was the keeper of the physical decrees. Agha Minas and Mukail's documentation was inside an all-silver tube-like cylinder to keep it safe. I hope we can access those documents one day, but I doubt it.

Agha Khacheeq Mecgrdeech

## Agha Khacheeq Mecgrdeech

Agha Khacheeq Mecgrdeech was a wealthy businessman with two daughters, Ossana and Tang Khatoon. His family had initially settled in Basra and then moved to Baghdad. Ossana met a captain, Stephen Lynch; they fell madly in love, but her father, Agha Khacheeq, forbade her from marrying the English captain. Captain Lynch left Baghdad, leaving his sweetheart behind. A few months passed, and Agha Khacheeq passed away, leaving the path open for Ossana to marry. She wrote a letter to her captain, and soon enough, he came back and married her, moving her to England.

Agha Khacheeq left his daughters very wealthy and had strong ties with the British Residency, which oversaw British interests since he worked there and was awarded British nationality for his services. He was the vice counsel for the British Residency in Baghdad. It is probably through the British Residency and his substantial activities in Basra that Captain Lynch, who had business ventures in mind, and Agha Khacheeq developed a relationship and met Ossana. On 10 November 1859, Ossana and Captain Lynch married. In the same year, he founded the London and Baghdad Banking Association. He used connections to obtain the sole right to navigate the Euphrates and Tigris rivers and to maintain two steamers on those rivers. Thomas Kerr Lynch and Stephen Lynch thus established the Euphrates and Tigris Steam Navigation Company and commissioned their steamers, even assisting in World War I. He established Stephen Lynch & Co. in Baghdad and Lynch Brothers & Co. in Basra as commodities traders.

Ossana Mecgrdeech Lynch

Ossana's mother-in-law, Rosa, was an Armenian too. She had married Robert Taylor at twelve and left her family in Shiraz. Also, the mother of Harriet, Ossana's daughter-in-law, was Armenian. Ossana never severed her ties with Baghdad, especially with her sister. Ossana's sister Tang Khatoon married Agha Mukail, who had bought land built using his father's and father-in-law's wealth and worked with his father in Baghdad's British Residency. Tang Khatoon sent her son to the U.K. to study and stay with his aunt. After a few weeks, Ossana sent a message saying he was having too good a time and should return home, which he did. The bond of this relationship remained unbreakable for generations; even when my mother, aunt, and uncle went to boarding schools in the U.K., the Lynch part of the family helped them find a suitable school. Many years later, the Lynch family welcomed another Armenian, Zagheek, the daughter of Aroos (Arousiak), into their family. Zagheek is my mother's paternal cousin. She was to be Malcolm Lynch's second wife.

Stephen Lynch and his children

As much as Ossana integrated into life in the U.K., she still held onto her language, traditions, and culture. One tale is that at Queen Victoria's court, Ossana presented her daughters. Ossana was a proud Armenian. She contacted her cousin; unfortunately, her sister was deceased by then (died in 1864), my mother's great-grandmother, and asked her to make Armenian clothes so they could also present their heritage at court. Eliza happily did so with great pride. She went to the best tailors, who had expensive materials embroidered and ordered for this special occasion.

Ossana Mecgrdeech Lynch

Ossana's daughters presented at Queen Victoria of
Britain dressed in traditional Armenian clothes.

# Blosse-Lynch
# Family Tree

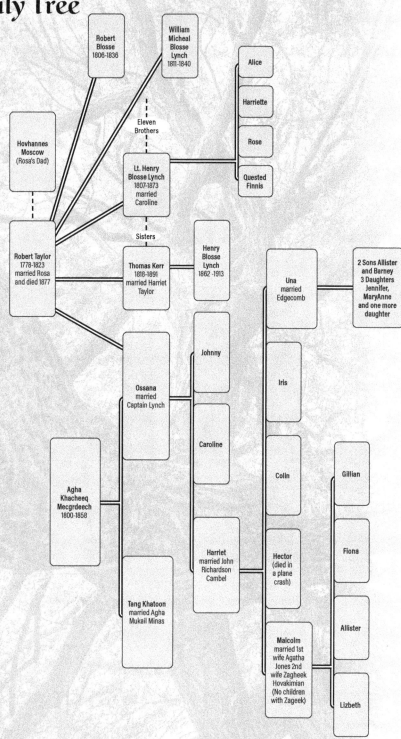

Robert Blosse 1806-1836

William Micheal Blosse Lynch 1811-1840

Alice

Harriette

Rose

Quested Finnis

Hovhannes Moscow (Rosa's Dad)

Eleven Brothers

Lt. Henry Blosse Lynch 1807-1873 married Caroline

Sisters

Robert Taylor 1778-1823 married Rosa and died 1877

Thomas Kerr 1818-1891 married Harriet Taylor

Henry Blosse Lynch 1862 -1913

Una married Edgecomb

2 Sons Allister and Barney 3 Daughters Jennifer, MaryAnne and one more daughter

Johnny

Iris

Ossana married Captain Lynch

Caroline

Colin

Gillian

Agha Khacheeq Mecgrdeech 1800-1858

Harriet married John Richardson Cambel

Hector (died in a plane crash)

Fiona

Allister

Tang Khatoon married Agha Mukail Minas

Malcolm married 1st wife Agatha Jones 2nd wife Zagheek Hovakimian (No children with Zageek)

Lizbeth

## Agha Minas and his Descendants Ventures

As I mentioned earlier, when he came from India with vast wealth, Agha Minas bought extensive properties, including Garara, an area in Baghdad. One lot was where the old American Embassy was. At first, my grandfather Vartan lived on Rasheed Street in Shorja. He built two bungalows in the orchard in Garara. My grandfather and his brother Minas were British and offered their land in 1917 so that the British troops could station themselves on this land in Muasker al Rasheed. Pre-1914, the Ottomans controlled Iraq and sided with Germany during the war. Over time, the descendants slowly started to sell off their shares. The vast wealth went to my grandfather Vartan and his brother Minas.

Minas was the first to sell a small portion of his land to Yacoub (Jacob) Yahuda, who changed Garara's name to Masbah. The roads needed excavations in Garara. Jacob Yahuda recommended that a small portion of the land be donated to the government to build a public swimming pool and a casino to generate traffic. It would help demonstrate the need to excavate the road to make transport accessible. His initiative was successful, including constructing a dam and paving the streets with a bus route, and this is how Garara became known as Masbah, as we know the area today.

Setrak, Agha Mukail's son, had married Mariam Tatossian; they had five children: Minas, Khatchig, Zabel, Aroos (Arousiak), and Vartan. Sadly, Khatchig died studying in India, causing his mother to be heartbroken since a letter asking for more money for his recovery never reached her while he was sick. In the 1910s, Hyke and his wife Zabel (my mother's aunt) lived in Annana, planting the vast land. When World War I broke out. Annana was associated with Hillah, which was under Ottoman rule. The Ottomans were on Germany's side. Zabel and Hyke went to hide in the desert with their two maids. They were lost for six months until her brother Minas, an Englishman, used his connections and located them. When he did so, they were in a desolate state.

The four were malnourished, skeleton-like in appearance, and very tanned. Zabel contracted T.B. For the next ten years, treating Zabel was a priority. Hyke went to Zabel's brother Minas and asked for help. Zabel then went to Lebanon with her maid Sarigool and her husband to receive treatment. They stayed there for ten years, leaving their daughter Lala to live with her Uncle Minas. When they returned, Lala used to call her birth parents Baba Hyke and Mama Zabel and Minas and his wife "Baba" and "Mama."

My paternal grandfather, Vartan, was an eligible bachelor who was the youngest of his siblings. He was a successful businessman and the brains of the family whose intentions were to move to France. He had spent many years there with his relatives. He married my grandmother

Vartan Minas

54

Arsina, a worthy catch of her day and a relative of his. She had striking blue eyes, a pale complexion, and light brown hair. She was a tall woman with a figure that most women envied. She also came from wealth and was a girl amongst three brothers. She was educated and fluent in four languages: Armenian, Arabic, English, and French. My grandfather, Vartan, often visited his uncles in France and spent time there. Unfortunately, his life was cut short, and he died of a heart attack in Ramallah on his way back from

Arsina Hovakimian

France. It was a time of war; with chaos and poor facilities, especially in summer, the decision to bury him there in Jerusalem seemed practical. His sister, Aroos, and his uncle's wife, Sarah Iskenderian, buried him there. He left three children under ten, which left my grandmother in a state of shock and despair. She wore black for the next ten years, mourning him.

## Family Travels

In the aftermath of the war, life slowly began to be put back together. Time is said to be a great healer. In my experience, the pain will always be there, but we learn to tolerate it. Indeed, there were also many joys in my family's life. My grandmother, mother, Aunt Nimette, Uncle Edmond, and their Uncle Vahe spent some summers in Lebanon, which was always fun for them. The summers in Lebanon were entertaining for the family. Rented accommodation was made available, with bedding and food sent ahead.

When they left Lebanon, they passed by Damascus in Syria. They would spend the night there and buy caramelized fruits, nuts, and dried fruit to return to Baghdad. On one of their holidays, they discovered they still needed to request a visa for my aunt, mother, and uncle to enter Baghdad because they were English. Previously, this was never an issue; no one had questioned them or seemed concerned. The primary way my family traveled at the time was via Nairn Transport, which conveyed travelers in trucks driven in sets of two.

The visa issue caused a dilemma until someone advised my grandmother and her brother Vahe to bribe the Nairn vehicle drivers to get around the problem of not having a visa and give them time for Vahe to get issued emergency visas. The plan was to ask the Iraqi Ambassador in Syria to issue an emergency visa. However, the ambassador was in Jordon for a funeral, which caused another problem. If they did not get an issued Iraqi visa, they would not be permitted access to cross the customs border of Iraq. Refusal of entry caused another issue: they had no Syrian-authorized travel permit, which was not an issue if you were an Iraqi but an issue if you were English.

Uncle Edmond, my mother, and my Aunt Nimette

My grandmother and her brother, faced with a significant dilemma, bribed the vehicle drivers to claim that one of the vehicles had a breakdown and needed a part and send the other truck ahead. The plan was underway, and Vahe boarded the vehicle that left. The next day, the "broken" part of the Nairn truck arrived with Vahe waiting at the border to hand over the urgently granted visas. After their father's death and that incident, my grandmother added them to her passport, and they were issued travel documents, but they did not have Iraqi nationality. Rules kept changing, with the government introducing new legislation forcing my mother, aunt, and uncle to apply for Iraqi nationality. It always surprised everyone that although my mother's family had been in Iraq for generations, they did not have Iraqi nationality. My mother only got it thanks to my father and not because she was part of a lineage born in Baghdad! It was not until the 1980s that my aunt and mother became Iraqi citizens.

Before Narin Transport, they traveled by convoy, which was easy prey to robbers. On one occasion, my mother's aunt, Aroos, and her children traveled that way, and on one of those journeys, robbers held up the convoy. My mother's cousin Araxi, a child then, began to cry. The robber asked why she was inconsolable. She had a new favorite blue dress, which she had bought in one of the trunks he was about to take. On hearing this, he instructed the family to take her trunk and return it to her. The robbers, robbing everything from everyone else but Araxi, filled the convoy's petrol tank just enough to get them to the next checkpoint. I find it amazing that the robbers were breaking the law, but at the same time, they showed compassion, understanding, and caring about getting their victims to safety.

## Contention Among Family

While we were all closely related, some issues and conflicts arose among family members. When Minas, my Grandfather Vartan's brother, died, he left no children but a wife, Eliza Iskenderian. His sisters, Zabel and Aroos, wanted the lion's share of his vast wealth and decided that the Iraqi probate and not the British probate should take effect. However, Minas and his wife were British, which took precedence by law as their nationality would determine what probate should be applied. It was customary since they were not Iraqi, which meant everyone would get a share: in the British probate, the wife takes precedence, and his sisters and his deceased brother would take a smaller share. The deceased man's family is prioritized should the Iraqi probate be enforced. Minas's sisters would take a more significant percentage, discriminating against my aunt and mother, who would not inherit anything since their father had passed away under Iraqi law; only my uncle is entitled. My mother and aunt are girls, prohibited from inheriting, yet their brother inherited since he was a boy.

They tricked my grandmother into hiring the same lawyer as theirs against their brother's wife, Eliza. They bribed officials and gained the right to make the Iraqi probate effective. When the lawyer admitted this to my grandmother, she was devastated since she was unaware of what was happening and had implicit trust in her sisters-in-law. This malicious act deeply upset my grandmother since she couldn't have dreamed that blood relatives would harm her girls, who had no father. That act cast a dark cloud over subsequent generations, even though my uncle married Aroos's granddaughter.

Growing up, I remember there were always issues, although we are closely related. I remember my grandmother being devastated because Zagheek, her husband's niece, took her to court because of the boundary wall between Zagheek's home and my grandmother's home. It was built inside Zagheek's land by less than a few inches, which is the builders' fault. The court papers were the first time my grandmother was aware of the situation and quickly resolved the matter. It would have been simple to mention it to my grandmother instead of going to court officially. Throughout the years, my mother, aunt, and grandmother stood by my uncle financially and morally, but for no reason, tensions always existed.

The incidents over the years are far too many and petty. We became distant due to them. My cousin from my father's side would mention the falling out between my maternal cousins amongst themselves and say, "Oh, it happens; money does this, and after a while, they will forgive each other and move on." It is ironic since my paternal cousin stood against us with the man who executed his brother: a murderer, a master forger, a liar, a thief, and a manipulator who only served his self-interest. I will discuss this story in the coming chapters, but needless to say, blood should be thicker than water.

I did try to forge a relationship with my maternal cousins, but it left me heartbroken. I found myself in the middle of hidden agendas and poor communication. They do not take ownership of their poor behavior, and accountability is nonexistent. New members of the family, through marriage, thought they had the right to mistreat us and disrespect us and get away with it; class and integrity have eluded them. After the last falling out, I decided to let things be. There is only a relationship if every person who is part of it is valued and respected. They said we were not close, but they had decided to make it so; this is on them. Communication is vital, and trust is essential. Without those, our relationship deteriorated. At this point, you hear about each other through strangers in passing, and in time, you become strangers, even weakening the ties further with your children until the bond ceases to exist.

In conclusion to this chapter, I would like to stress that communication is vital, especially in the family, and to apologize and move on makes us humble and vulnerable. It is a sign of strength, not weakness. Our ancestors came a long way in establishing themselves and flourishing. We live in different corners of the world now; there should be loyalty and respect. Family should celebrate our accomplishments and, at the same time, support each other through failures.

# Chapter 5

## Life in Baghdad

In this chapter, I want the reader to glimpse how we lived and came to be in Baghdad. I tried to introduce the culture and history tied to anecdotes and experiences I encountered; through stories of my family members and myself, I want to share experiences and give insight into life as an Armenian living in Baghdad.

Ever since I can remember, whether in society or even at school in Baghdad, I have identified as "Armenian Baghdadi." The "Armenian Baghdadis," my ancestors, did not suffer from the 1915 genocide at the hands of the Turks. They had settled in Iraq as far back as the 1600s, a land they subsequently were born in for generations. Like other minority groups, they were always labeled as outsiders and clung to the Armenian identity, in which they had great pride. All marriages were within the

group; the church in Armenia, Etchimiadzin, where our headquarters is, even granted permission for first cousins to marry,
but not paternal. However, the church later revoked the decision significantly when the community grew. When it came
to marriage, Armenians rarely married outside of their ethnic
race. It created a scandal and was frowned upon, making them
outcasts. My father's maternal aunt said, "Irak'i hay kám tsur
e, kám tsurrn," meaning an "Armenian Iraqi is either crazy or
crooked" due to the intermarriages.

The Iraqi Armenians settled in two districts of Baghdad,
Medan, and Shorja. My father's family was from the Medan
district, and my mother's family settled in Shorja. Shorja's settlers were the elite, those who had money. The Medan settlers
were more working class.

At the turn of the 19th century, the Armenian settlers in
Iraq lived in houses called "shanasheel," where the windows in
front of the home almost touched each other, with the street
separating them. In the afternoons, they sat on the balconies
and chatted. Baskets would be lowered from the balconies so
the salesman could put the goods into the basket hoisted up.
It was a close-knit community. It centered around their home,
relatives, and friends, with the church playing a pivotal role.

Athamia "shanasheel" 1930 by Arsen Hovakimian

The women were the backbone of the family. It was they who orchestrated and controlled family life. The women mainly stayed at home, and the men worked. The women married much older men and often survived them, strengthening the maternal influence and the children bonding more with their maternal side.

There were no coffee shops or restaurants where the women could gather, so their only option was to get together at each other's homes or venture out for gatherings at churches and schools, including for significant events like Christmas, Easter, and Name Days. Annana was a frequent venue, and picnics and hunting were also a part of my family's activities.

Cher Ali Cherchef – what the Armenians wore
instead of the customary Arab abaya

The Armenian community stayed together and socialized together. When the Armenian women did go out, they wore an abaya called "Cher Ali Chercheft." The abaya was a piece of cloth that covered their heads and bodies. It went down to their ankles. Unlike the black abayas of the Arabs, the abaya worn by the Armenians was a colorful, elaborately embroidered fabric that women wore. After their death, the family often donated it to the church. They used to make a chasuble out of it for the priest to wear during mass.

Picnic in Taq Kasra c.1920

On their way to an Armenian gathering c.1920

Selection of Family and Friends Activities

Zagheek Markarian

Family Activities 1930s -1950s

A musician is playing an instrument in Tak Kasra.

 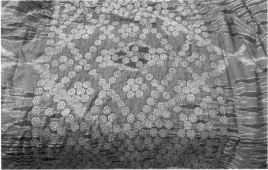

Bath peshtemal, pumice stone, and loofah

Going to the Turkish bath (at Al Naher Street) during my grandmother's era was customary. The towel or wrap (called a peshtemal), typically worn to the bath and other bathing necessities, is part of a bride's marriage chest. The bath necessities are elaborate. They are embroidered or even have metal sewn onto them like silver. You have the peshtemal, the loofah, a glove made of the same material as the peshtemal, and a pumice stone used for the skin. My mother's family had their Turkish bath in their home. Unfortunately, the Turkish bath caused a horrific fire, burning my grandfather's prized Persian carpet collection.

I asked my mother to describe the floor plan to understand how they lived, which is so different from what we are used to now. I find it interesting that in the basement, they had a "cold room," or "serdab," as they referred to it, that had a windcatcher or "badgir" with a chimney attached that ventilated it. I find it incredible that they stored rice and flour for months there, yet I can't keep such items with the latest technology for a fraction of the time!

In the hot summer weather, they used a hose with holes on top of the windows to keep the house cooler and hang "aagool," a desert bush with thorns. The water would drip on it, and the window opened, forming a breeze to enter the home. Their

Aagool put at the windows to keep cool.

house was that of her grandmother, Zagheek. She inherited it from her mother, Eliza, who owned the two shops beside it. One was a convenience store she rented to a man named Phillip, and the other was a stationary/bookstore. The house no longer belongs to us since it paid her death duty.

My mother's grandmother, Zagheek

In the 1930s, after several generations of living there, the house was two stories with a courtyard centered in the middle of the house. A toilet, servant quarters, kitchen, and Turkish bath were adjacent to a furnace room on the ground floor. A dining room and a living room are also on the same floor. The living room had French windows overlooking the river, and the fridge was there. There was also a divider to make the large room smaller if needed. There is a small storage room to store food in the living room. The bedrooms, bathrooms, and summer dining room were on the first floor. Later, in 1940, my uncle was given his room by building an extension from my grandmother's room. The "Kapashcam," or cold room, another storage space, was located up the stairs from the courtyard on the first floor. In summer, they slept on the roof to enjoy a colder environment.

Pre-1915, the Armenian community was not as big as it was to become, which meant more interaction with the Arabs and the English through everyday life, which led to the community's fluency in Arabic and English. As I said earlier, the Armenian language has no masculine or feminine, which causes some Armenian people to confuse masculine and feminine terms in other languages that distinguish the sexes. However, you would rarely find an Armenian from that era or their descendants whose masculinity and femininity are not indicated clearly in Arabic or English, thanks to the fluency in these languages caused by proximity to these peoples.

In 1915, all Armenian families helped those who had escaped the genocide settle in Baghdad. They either supported them in setting them up in businesses and trade or employed them in their households or businesses. There was no segregation between servants and employers, as in the western homes. Servants were seen as part of the family and were married off and set up.

The home my mother grew up in overlooked the river

The home my mother grew up in from a different angle

My grandmother's home, where my mother grew up,
was on Rasheed Street facing Hasso Brothers.

When my mother was still a child, her relatives lived nearby.
The children returned from school, and on holidays, they used

to be in and out of each other's houses. One of their neighbors was Manaheem Daniel. My mother told me that, said to her, he descended from Daniel, a biblical figure, and still, until then, had owned his ancestor's land near Babylon, Chefel.

After school, my uncle's favorite pastime was using his pellet gun to hunt birds. It was also the siesta hour for Mr. Daniel, as it was for most, especially with the heat. Mr. Daniel made a deal with the kids to play with his elevator, a novelty set in his home, if they promised to stay quiet during the siesta hour. The kids saw this as the ultimate treat since, at that time, elevators were rare, especially in private homes. It was a deal the kids could not refuse. Mr. Daniel's nephew lived a little further down the road and owned a one-seater plane, another playing venue for the kids.

Wherever we came to settle after immigrating from Baghdad, we had a love of orchards, a nostalgia brought down from one generation to the next. This love went as far back as the era of Agha Minas. He set the orchards around his palace. Later, bungalows were built in Garara, nine kilometers south of Baghdad, replacing the palace, and every fruit was grown there. The Arab farmers were crossbreeding different fruits like oranges and lemons during pollination. The orchards slowly depreciated in size in the future generations since the land was divided and sold.

Our homes went into the Tigris River, and my parents learned to swim there. In my parents' time, each child had a Jewish swimming instructor. My grandmother used to sit in the boat while they swam across the river and back. In the summers, they used to sleep on the roof since it was so hot. For most of the summer, they went to Lebanon and later Europe. Life was simple but also very rich.

Arsen Hokakimian 1931 (My mother's uncle)

As I mentioned, picnics, Annana being a frequent venue, and gatherings, whether in the church, schools, or the Armenian club, were part of life. My grandfather Vartan loved to organize picnics and even venture out hunting. The Armenian community stayed together and socialized together. I included some pictures from 1930 around Baghdad taken by Arsen Hovakimian.

Abou Serfen and Bazaar Serfen 1930 by Arsen Hovakimian

Abou Serfen and Bazaar Serfen 1930 by Arsen Hovakimian

Adamiah Selaikh 1930 by Arsen Hovakimian

Adamiah Selaikh 1930 by Arsen Hovakimian

Customs House 1930 by Arsen Hovakimian

Emek-Khanah Street 1930 by Arsen Hovakimian

Exchange Square 1930 by Arsen Hovakimian

Haidar Khana Tomb New Street Rasheed Street 1930 by Arsen Hovakimian

General Hospital Street 1930 by Arsen Hovakimian

General Hospital Street 1930 by Arsen Hovakimian

The first Iraqi pilots to come by five airplanes from London
on April 22, 1931, at 6 p.m. by Arsen Hovakimian.

King Faisal arriving from Europe on October 1, 1930

King Faisal arriving from Europe on October 1, 1930

The street of Bab Al-Sherqi to Kerada -Hindia The
road of the old bridge, June 19, 1930

The street of Bab Al-Sherqi to Kerada-Hindia The
road of the old bridge, June 19, 1930

Education had been essential for the Armenian people. The girls went to study at the nun's school, known as "Rahibat," meaning "Presentation Sisters." They educated four generations in my family. My mother's grandmother, Zagheek, her daughter Arsina, my mother, aunt, and I were all under their care.

I spent my early years in Switzerland. I arrived in Baghdad at two, and the kindergarten accepted me. I wouldn't say I liked school; it horrified me. My whole world turned upside down. It terrified me because my previous playgroup in Switzerland was the neighbor's children, and I felt secure and had fun. In this school, I thought I was too alone to fend for myself, and the staff was aggressive, prioritizing discipline. It felt regimented, put under the microscope every second of the day. I had little in common with my classmates, who knew nothing better. I often cried, and Kafy, the playground supervisor, used to take care of me.

We studied Arabic, French, and English, and I took piano lessons. Hertz, a German-Austrian piano teacher, taught piano in my mother's time. Ballet and singing were also part of the curriculum. I am good at many things, but music has never been an area in which I excelled; in fact, I failed. My worst nightmare was piano lessons. If I relaxed and rested my hands on the keyboard, my teacher would wack me with a ruler. She hit me too hard on a particular day, and my eyes swelled up, and my hands burned. I looked at her in horror, ran out of the room, and smacked into Reverend Mother Jean. She looked at me, and fear overtook me as I looked at her. The nuns dressed in layers and layers of white, everything crisply ironed with starch, making sure the pleats were sharp and perfect, with a black habit on their heads, but all I could see was this giant white marshmallow in front of me, so I grabbed her hand and sunk my teeth, biting her. At the main office, I waited for my mother with Lena Shukur, the office secretary; her parents were my parents' friends, who consoled me. My mother came in. The Reverend Mother told her, "As I walked the corridors, you used to fear me and would not dare utter a word. She took revenge on behalf of all of you".

On leaving the school, a tall man from Sudan used to sell roasted peanuts outside of the school gates, the best I have ever had! They were almost burnt but not entirely, and the amount sold made you want more. He used to put them in a newspaper swirled like a cone.

Me

My mother and aunt with the Catholicos; I never got a picture!

After a few years, I changed schools to learn Armenian at the Armenian Catholic School. Sister Zarouhi was designated to teach me Armenian; she was wonderful. I remember the Catholicos from Yerevan, Armenia, were to visit Baghdad, and the task of presenting him with a bouquet and reciting a short speech fell on me. I would stay after school, and Sister Zarouhi would coach me. My reward for working hard was going to the kitchen and getting the most delicious bread the Reverand Mother baked. The speech went perfectly, thanks to Sister Zarouhi's hard work and patience. I gave the address in the VIP section of the airport, where they welcomed the Catholicos. Security was extremely tight, and photographs were not allowed. However, the news that evening did cover the event and showed a clip of me presenting the bouquet.

I presented flowers to Addis Harmandian, the Armenian singer.

At another time, I was fortunate to be selected to present the singer Addis with a bouquet at the end of his concert in Baghdad. My first concert!

The nuns were marvelous and dedicated to catching me up in Armenian. On the first day of school, Sister Kayane met me, and she took me to a girl and said, "She will look after you; her name is also Tania." For some strange reason, until then, I did not speak Armenian. However, I understood Iraqi Armenian perfectly since my mother conversed with her family in Armenian, and my father with his sister and mother. Still, my parents communicated with each other in Arabic. The group of friends I had there was delightful; through Facebook, destiny would intervene, and we were in touch forty years later.

On our way back from school, there used to be a bakery up the street from where we lived in Masbah. In the window, they displayed sponge cakes with decadent cream on the top, experiencing the blistering heat for days. I used to beg my mother to buy a piece, and sometimes, she indulged me. Thanks to that, I have an iron-clad stomach. I sometimes was treated with ice cream in the afternoons, given my sweet tooth. There used to be a place with the most delicious apricot ice cream. The Ministry of Health, at intervals, used to conduct health checks. Whenever they tested the level of bacteria in the ice cream, the results indicated deficient levels of bacteria. The results baffled everyone. The results led to an investigation, and they found out the owner mixed antibiotics with the ice cream—another contributing factor to my steel-proof stomach.

In my St. George's School uniform

In the same way as my parents, I studied abroad to continue my education. When I was nine, I attended a boarding school in the U.K., St. George's Ascot. Being sent away to study was not the norm, especially at nine years old, yet my parents felt I would get a better standard of education in the U.K. They hoped it would practice other educational methods than memorization, which the Iraqi educational system teaches us. The major challenge was learning a new language and building my vocabulary to express myself better; I could not apply critical thinking skills and research options to solve problems. Conflict resolution and empathy were all new to me. I had to reprogram myself at nine years old.

When the Armenians first arrived, their survival and heritage preservation was paramount. The Armenian priests taught them the Armenian language and the Bible. In 1848, two Armenians traveled to study in Edjmiadzin (the Armenian church headquarters in Armenia). Baghdassar Davitian (Mesorb Davitian) studied Theology, and Manuel Dilanian studied the Armenian language. Davitian was ordained as a priest and was buried at the Holy Trinity in 1892, while Dilanian became certified as a teacher. Supreme Vartabet Mesorb established the Armenian school Sourp Takmanechatz Varjaran (School of the Holy Translator) by raising funds. Dilanian was the headmaster.

However, the Armenian boys later attended another school since it provided a better, broader curriculum. The boys' school was Al Najah, with the principal and owner Qawmi. Later, the Jesuits' Baghdad College welcomed the boys. That is where my father and uncles attended. When it came to my cousins, they attended Saint Joseph School. At seven years old, on weekends, my mother took my cousin Rafi and me to study French from Sister Mubaraka—another nightmare.

At the same time, my mother decided I should start piano lessons again, but this time with a private Russian teacher. She was so patient, but I had no love for the piano. Sometimes, I followed the lessons given to Hagop Chobanian, who was very talented and pursued his piano education in the U.K. At five o'clock, you would hear the most beautiful music that bewitched you, courtesy of Hagop, and at six o'clock, you would wish to lose your sense of hearing, courtesy of myself.

Sometimes, on our way to my piano lesson, we would pass by a department store, "Alat and Dakika," and shop. The government would import random goods sold at very reasonable prices, which it controlled and monitored. On one occasion, we saw Rolex pocket watches selling for seemingly five dinars. However, the display price was wrong. The intended price was fifty dinars, but the zero, presented as a dot when written in Arabic, was forgotten by the vendor, and people bought them at five dinars instead of fifty, either thinking they were fake or not appreciating their actual value. Another store that sold government-priced goods was "Arosdibag." Sometimes, you would pass by and see a long lineup and queue up just for the hell of it because you know you would buy a bargain.

Lining up at the department store would always be an adventure; either you would bond with the people you were queueing with, or fights would break out; there was always a story to tell. On one occasion, the maids told my mother they heard tea kettles sold on a particular day, and they wanted one. My mother took them and waited outside as they prepared for "combat." You have no opportunity to choose a color or style; you randomly take what the salesperson gives you. While waiting outside, my mother saw a lady selling them at a profit. She decided to buy two. Our maids came out haggard and worn out with no kettles. My mother casually held the two kettles, and the maids' eyes lit up as she handed them over. Whenever I see a queue, something inside me urges me to join.

Education in my family has been essential and valued. Family members travel abroad to get the best education whenever possible. However, it was a rarity during my time since Iraq was becoming a dictatorship, and travel was very restricted. My grandfather's maternal uncle was the Patriarchate in Constantinople; for the boys on my Grandfather's maternal side, the Patriarch made education possible in Istanbul.

Many Armenians studied abroad, whether in the United Kingdom or India. On both maternal and paternal sides were graduates of India and some even Turkey. Those countries at the time were considered the best educational venues, and many Armenians went to them, including my mother's Uncle Arsen, my father's Uncle Leon, and Skender Tatossian. My mother's uncle Vahe and the generation that followed them went to study in Birmingham, United Kingdom. At the same time, their friend (also a relative), Dr. Setrak, studied in Edinburgh, Scotland. My father's maternal aunt, Mari Abrahamian, graduated from Leicester University, and her brother, Edward Abrahamian, graduated from a U.K. school in Optometry. Like my father and mother, the following generation went to study mainly in the United Kingdom, Europe, and the United States. I found some old pictures of school class portraits and gatherings in Baghdad that would give a better idea of the times in Baghdad. I wrote the names of those we can recognize; if you know of someone unidentified, please let me know, and I will add their name.

We recognize the person in the 4th row, 4th from the left, as Armina Stephan, 2nd row, 2nd from the right Victoria Abrahamian, 1st row, 3rd from the right as Araxi Hovakimian.

1st row, second from the right, Syran Dablamian (Yeprem's wife sold cloth), Archbishop Roupen Minasian Serpazan, in the middle. 2nd row 4th from the right Victoria Abrahamian. The little boy with the diploma to the left is Vahram Aardoun.

Sitting 3rd from the right, Ovanes Hovakimian (my mother's grandfather).
Second row, 4th from the right, Marcar Hovakimian (Ovnanes's
brother and husband to my mother's paternal aunt Aroos)

Mrs. Stout School: 1st row from left:. 2nd Anna Ovanessian, 3rd Araxi
Ovanessoff, 4th Alice Iskenderian, 5th Elize Iskenderian (John Gourje)
2nd row from left:. 3rd and 4th are teachers 5th Mrs. Stout, a teacher.
8th Arsina Hovakimian 3rd row from left:. 3rd Dzaghig Ovanesoff.

April 1939 Umm Atham Gathering of Armenian Iraqi

1. Mary Tatossian
2. Zagheek Hovekimian
3. Elize Ovanesoff
4. Sirvart Topalian
5. Eugene Papsian(Stephan)
6. Meline Iskenderian
7. Percy Tatossian
8. Araxi Hovekimian
9. Sophie Tatossian
10. Edma Tatossian
11. Anahid Topalian
12. Sarah
Tatossian Khachanian
13. Makrouhi Tatossian
(Evelyn's mother)
14. Hermoir Koumjjian
(Hagop's mother)
15. Mrs. Turabian
16. -
17. Mrs. Beoyian
18. Zaven Badriak
19. Mother (Afnefe)
20. Agavni Parpirian

21. FR Soukiassian
22. Barkevr Babikian
23. Markerit Melconian
24. Eliza Iskenderian
25. Zabel Boghosian
(Anton's mother)
26. Mary Bedrosian
27. Torabian
28. Stephan Hovakimain
29. Arousiak Charkarian
30. Daigik Hovnanian
31. Ekmehjan (wife of Orkan)
32. Toros Kevenjian
(Hagop's father)
33. Mrs. Topalian
34. -
35. Roxana Boghosian
36. Markerit Boghosian
(Boghos Bogosian's wife)
37. Takouhi Atachian
38. Minas Minas
39. Alexon Derughian
40. Hampersoun Atchean

41. Dr. Najib Babikian
42. Setrak Boghosian
43. -
44. Ohanes Melkonian
45. Kasbar Boghosian
46. Dr. Bedros Bedrosian
47. Ardarhis Megerdian
48. Haig Seropian
49. Dr. Muktarian
(Ekimehjian's wife's brother)
50. Abcar Ovanesian
51. Dekran Ekimehjian
52. Dr. Topalian
53. Garabet Melkonian
54. Skender Stephan
55. Mamook Tatossian
56. Boghos Boghosian
57. Arsen Kedour
58. Levon Shishmanian
59. Stephan Iskenderian
60. Farogh

The household I grew up in consisted of anecdotes, story-telling, and references to the past. I have included some of my favorites. I want the reader to feel what life was like at the time.

One story is of my mother's paternal aunt and my maternal grandmother buying Bally suede shoes; my grandmother's was smaller. My mother's aunt, Zabel, wore out her shoes and went to her sister-in-law, Arsina. She explained to her family that, as worn out as the shoes were, she couldn't part with them—they were too comfortable, and she couldn't replace them, as this kind of shoe was now unavailable. My grandmother told her she could have hers, which she had not worn yet. At that, my mother's aunt demanded a bucket of warm water and wore the shoes, squeezing her feet in and putting them in the bucket until they expanded, and took them home.

In another incident, one sister, my mother's aunt, Aroos, went to the dentist and needed dentures. She was so happy with the outcome and told her sister, Zabel, that she too should have dentures, although there was nothing wrong with her teeth, as the dentist was so professional and his work of high quality and that he was getting old and may not be around. The sister listened to her and went and had dentures made, too!

On Iraq Television, there was a play whereby a widower would go and talk to his dead wife, for whom he had built a shrine in his bedroom. The play continued for a while, with most households holding their breath until the next episode. A picture of the dead wife appears in the last episode of the series. The photo was of my mother's cousin, Zagheek, who had been taken years before by a renowned photographer in Baghdad in my grandparents' and parents' time. Iraq TV often would look at his archive for vintage photographs.

When my parents were young, people would visit each other's homes more. Club activities, such as "Nadi al Alwia," or the Armenian Club, provided entertainment and a venue for people to get together. When I lived in Baghdad as a child, I remember Nadi al Alwia showing films outside for children on Thursday evenings, which was a treat. The Disney movie *Peter Pan* was a constant. During my parent's time, they had access to an open-air theater named Diana, where they watched films from the balcony of relatives who lived next to the theater.

All my mother's side of the family, including us, lived in Masbah. Often, my grandmother would walk me to the river edge, where there was a boundary fence to keep out intruders. The water frequently flooded the garden, but this did not happen in the later years—a dam built further up the river dried up the soil, forming cracks in the ground. My grandmother would look across the river at the oil refinery's flame and share, as the dry heat touched her skin, where the wind was blowing from and what the weather would be. Despite all the riches the country was experiencing, the people's souls, like the ground, were slowly drying up.

This is how I will always remember Grandmother Arsina.

I have heard that the sense of smell stays in your memory the longest. I remember that in all our houses were bushes of "Rasqui," a flower from the Jasmine family. You would smell it as you entered the house, taking your breath away. As you entered the garden from the deck at my grandmother's home, it would intoxicate you.

There were two other major household events whose experience and smell always stayed with me. The first occurred twice a year. These Eastern Turkish (Turkoman) men who used to be the porters at the "Hasso Iquan" department store came to our home. Their ability to carry heavy things was beyond human capability. The head was a man who went by the name of Challawi. He knew four generations of my family. As a child, he knew my grandmother's mother; as an older man, he knew me.

They used to come every spring and every autumn to tend to the Persian carpets. They spread them out in the garden courtyard, washed them, carried them three stories up, and spread them out on the roof to dry. Once they were dry, they returned the following day and either spread them in the home or stored them with "babonag" (a herb from the mint family) to protect them from moths. A big Goa chest with gold metal designs greeted you at the entrance. This massive chest, which needed ten men to move, was the wedding chest of my mother's grandmother, Eliza, the oldest in her family. It stored Persian carpets in the summers, and you could faintly smell the babonag as you passed. During the fall of Saddam, looters destroyed the chest; they decided to destroy it because they couldn't take it out because of its size and weight.

The other significant activity was extracting rose water. Heaps and heaps of rose petals would carpet our long driveway. The vision of mountains of rose petals and the pungent smell will always stay with me. The "Wared Al Jury," the flower used to extract the rose water, was only sold for approximately three days a year. Invariably, the first extract bottle was the strongest and most valuable. Because my family considered them unlucky, we have never owned the pots for this—the relatives of my grandmother or my mother's paternal aunt would lend theirs.

Another memory is that a man would visit and sell us Damascus berries once a year. He would weigh it on an old-fashioned scale, and as soon as he left, you could see the ground stained from the berries. His mark stayed for months. I also remember the man who came round and sold us oil from a large metal carriage pulled by a horse. Someone was always visiting to offer a service, whether selling oil, fruits, or even shining shoes.

Throughout the year, there was always some activity. The activities centered around preserving particular products available at that time of year or maintaining the home somehow. Making jam and concentrated juices from different fruits was always on the list. Only the best was available and displayed at feasts like Christmas, Name Days, Easter, and my birthday. Those smells, the emotions, and the excitement will forever stay with me, engraved in my memory. It breaks my heart to know my children will never have access to such experiences or have insight into such a life, a life that soon would be forgotten. Yet, I feel so fortunate to have been exposed to such a prosperous life.

# Chapter 6

## Sarah Iskenderian

This chapter will discuss Sarah Iskenderian, a relative of mine and a fairly well-known figure in Iraq. Sarah Iskenderian was Iraq's "poor little rich girl." Her story occurred at the turn of the twentieth century—a time of significant change and progress. She is my mother's cousin. This chapter is the most challenging piece to write about in this book. It is mainly because of references to Sarah's story in other literature, television series, and documentaries. Most people seem to have an opinion of her. She is even considered an exemplary "proverb" as a precautionary tale. "You can be filthy rich like Sarah and still die a pauper." I have heard this countless times and feel my sarcasm wedging in. It surprises me how many people have seen her wearing no hat and clogs in the blistering heat at a bus stop. My favorite of these sayings is, "With all the money in the world, you can still be unhappy; look at Sarah." It saddens me that Sarah is not given the respect due to her, especially since she did a great deal of good and was let down by many. She did inherit colossal wealth, but the times and people around her made her a prime target.

Sarah was never a pauper and had a relatively happy life, and in her later years, she lived modestly like most people. Money makes life easier, and living without it strains any relationship. However, it causes greed and envy, whether rich or poor, especially among those around you. It causes insecurity if you do not have it; if you do, you fear losing it because it can be part of your identity.

In whatever way people refer to her, it is a testament to her existence, and even after all these years, she will remain a tragic figure in Iraq's history. She did a great deal of good for the Armenian community. She donated plots of land, one of which is "Camp Sarah," to serve her community. Most prominent Armenian families donated to their community and church, but their donations were more discreet. Tax exemptions also supported them when donating to the church. Lately, I have identified with her more; some aspects of her story have made no sense to me, but by empathizing with the situation and considering the times and her relatives and community, I understand her more. The betrayal and abandonment by her relatives, her cousin, and her uncle, and the lack of support from even the people close to her caused her harm, is something we have had to live through as of late. The psychological scars of facing such things run deep and change our outlook on life.

Before its production for Iraq Television, the television series caused much anguish to her daughters, Sophie and Edma. Someone had contacted Sophie before her passing, but she did not want to participate in the production. The series moved forward only after her children's deaths, leaving no direct descendants but us to challenge it. Some facts are offensive and skewed, but the storyline probably had to take that route for dramatic effect. However, her true story is even more captivating.

I decided to document her story from the perspective of her daughter, Edma. Edma, my mother's cousin, lived in London, U.K., before passing—a lady in every sense with a great deal of dignity and pride. My grandfather, Edma's cousin, gave her that name. Later, my grandfather named his daughter (my mother) Edma because he loved the name so much. Edma married Edward Romanoski (Teddy), a Polish-Prussian nobleman. She often visited my mother, and both would sit for hours recounting stories about Baghdad and gossiping about the whole family, reminiscing about the "good old days." The story of her mother would often come up. I was oblivious to its importance as part of Iraq's heritage when I was young. Her mother's story feels like it comes from *One Thousand and One Nights*, full of tragedy, love, and betrayal.

As I grew older and she visited, I started paying more attention to Sarah's story and asking more questions. I could not understand why Sarah was so vulnerable—where was her mother's side of the family (my family) to protect her? I have found answers to those questions through my experiences in the last ten years. Edma and Sophie were paranoid and suspicious of everyone; the only person Edma trusted implicitly was my mother. The reason for her suspicion is simple: the men closely related to her from her mother's side were too young to take on any responsibility or wanted not to get involved. Her uncle Setrak died before her mother. My mother's uncle Minas did not help anyone, including my mother and her siblings, when his brother passed away, and there were financial issues between himself and his siblings. It also did not help that he later married Sarah's uncle's (Sayrop) daughter, Eliza. My grandfather Vartan was a child. On her father's side, they extorted her.

These trust issues stemmed from too many people backstabbing Sarah's family for their self-interest. The main enemy was within her own family. The family characteristics and dynamics haven't changed. Examining the family history and the ease of granting forgiveness with little lawful consequences set a poor example. It keeps happening. They prefer not to stand by each other if there is no common interest but would never sever ties, as it could affect their popularity or lead to opposition. Jealousy and self-preservation were the number one priority. Loyalty and integrity amongst each other are not part of their lives.

Sarah Iskenderian was born in Baghdad in 1889 to Sophie Minas and Ohanes Iskenderian. She was the middle child of three. Sadly, her brother Kayrob died in infancy, and her sister Zabel passed away very young. Ohanes donated a considerable sum in Zabel's honor to the Armenian Orthodox Church to serve the Armenian people. Ohanes also built an Armenian school to honor his deceased child the Zabelian School.

Sophie, born in 1856, was wealthy in her own right. She had inherited vast wealth from her mother, Tang Khatoon, and her father, Agha Mukail. When Sophie's father, Agha Mukail, passed away, she and her two sisters, who had both married and left for Istanbul, stole the deeds to Agha Mukail's properties upon his death. This action cut out their brother Setrak, my mother's paternal grandfather, from his inheritance. Agha Mukail's sister, Mariam, was upset with them. She had lost her husband and children in the black plague and decided to give Setrak all of her wealth and exclude her nieces, making up for her nieces' evil deeds.

As you can see, they were strong women who acted vindictively. I believe in Karma—if you do a terrible act or wrong, then it gets paid back to you or through your children. Family history has demonstrated this time and time again.

Sarah had a sense of entitlement but not to the same level as her mother. Sophie and her two sisters, the daughters of Agha Mukail, were so arrogant and self-righteous that they terrorized Armenian society with their imposed self-worth. They expected royal treatment wherever they went; even designated chairs were available in the church, ensuring no one else could sit on them.

Sarah, her mother, Sophie, and her sister Zabel

Ohanes, Sarah's father, had great wealth through his wife and business activities, enabling him to work with the Ottoman governor of Baghdad, the "Wali." Thanks to Wali's connections, he and Ohanes could buy land being repossessed and resold at a low price by banks and lending authorities. He also worked on other ventures with the Wali. The governor's position was sensitive, so they purchased the properties and put them in Ohanes' name. By default, Ohanes inherited this vast wealth upon Wali's death despite being already wealthy.

Sarah's mother died when she was six years old in 1895. Her paternal aunt, Sophie, came to live with her father and look after Sarah. She helped arrange for Sarah's education. It seemed out of character because Sarah is my grandmother's age (they are cousins), and all the girls were treated the same and kept together. The community was small for their survival; being an ethnic minority, the family was very close, especially where the girls were concerned.

In my great-grandmother's generation, the nuns at the Presentation Sisters educated my grandmother, who spoke English, French, Arabic, and Armenian. Yet, Sarah was not so fluent in all those languages. However, according to her daughter, Sarah attended school for some time.

A common practice in our homes was that Armenian servants served inside the home, and Sarah's maid was Armanuhi. The servants are like members of the family. Those outside the house, like the guards and gardeners, were Arabs. Arabic was used to communicate; the Iraqi Armenians speak Arabic better than the genocide survivors because they mixed more with the Arab population and learned Arabic from them.

Sara lost her father before reaching the legal age of twenty-one. He passed away in 1899, leaving Sarah an orphan at ten. Thus, she inherited vast wealth from her parents at ten years old.

After the death of Sarah's father, a guardian had to be appointed. The church appointed Sayrop as her guardian since he was her paternal uncle. The church regarded Sayrop as the closest male to the girl other than her father. Thus, her astronomical wealth was at his disposal for a considerable time. Since he was family, it was unthinkable that she would prosecute him for stealing a substantial amount from her wealth; emotional ties and the family's reputation were at stake. It is hard to judge unless you are in such a situation, and reality hits you; as bold as you are, as much of a victim as you are, and though you may have ample evidence, you become paralyzed. One account states that Sayrop wanted her to marry his nephew, Daniel, Kevork's son, so her wealth stayed at his disposal indefinitely. I find that difficult to believe since there is a twenty-year difference between them, and our church did not allow paternal cousins to marry. However, relatives consider themselves entitled by default.

So, Sayrop and his nephew, Daniel, took advantage of Sarah's wealth without consequence. Sarah was a poor businesswoman and very spoilt. Unfortunately, as a woman in Baghdad, her hands are tied. The women in my family are strong, educated women. However, when you live in an environment with clipped wings and very little support, you are disabled, giving the men the upper hand. As a young woman like Sarah living in that part of the world, with your education based on being a lady and not life or business skills, you are easy prey to strangers, especially your family. They feel more entitled than anyone else to take advantage of you, and jealousy gives them a sense of contentment with your suffering.

There is no debate that Sarah was wealthy and inherited vast wealth, but often, it is exaggerated. I have heard accounts that state that for over an hour by train, you can ride from one boundary of her vast estate to the other; another exaggerated assessment of her wealth is that she owned one-fifth of Iraq.

The Garden of Eden is said to exist on her land if you don't believe in the mythological meaning of the garden.

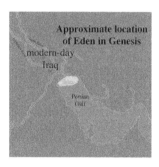

The Garden of Eden, the biblical garden believed to be on Sarah's Land

During one of her visits, I asked Edma about the Garden of Eden being on her mother's property. I looked up the location of the Garden of Eden, and sure enough, it was on land that Sarah had owned. On her next visit, one of the pictures Edma gave to my mother was of Sarah standing in front of a tree surrounded by a low brick boundary, and she stated that they believed that that was the tree of the forbidden fruit. Later, she passed my mother things like stories, accounts, and memorabilia. The attic of my parent's home housed a box containing those for twenty years. Only during the pandemic did I have time to sort through those journals, letters, diaries, and pictures. I hope future generations can enjoy them.

Sarah next to the forbidden tree at the claimed Garden of Eden

Having great wealth also comes with great responsibility: maintaining, respecting, and utilizing it to flourish. Sarah had the world at her feet, with dark looks and a charming personality. Besides having no responsibilities, she was spoilt and had a fiery temper, and her uncle manipulated her and extorted her. She knew that to escape from his clutches, she needed an ally and to gain support from someone above him. Society, however, dictated that for an Armenian girl to go and seek help from such a man directly was scandalous, but on the other hand, no one helped.

In 1910, at seventeen, Sarah attended a party with her aunt Sophie (who shared Sarah's mother's name); most of her social circle consisted of Armenians, most of whom were related to her, and the British. There were strong ties with the British since her ancestors had worked with them and were British nationals and British relatives.

It was a party attended by society's elite with many dignitaries—the newly appointed Ottoman governor of Baghdad, Hussain Nadim Pasha, was also present. Sarah charmed Hussain and decided to approach him to help her get rid of her uncle's guardianship.

She and her aunt went the next day to see him. He was smitten and admired this feisty seventeen-year-old who had the guts to come and see him. He listened to her and agreed to help her. He ordered Sarah's accounts to be submitted to his office and told her he would audit them within twenty-four hours. She has regained her right to run her business independently. To her delight, Sarah could finally manage her wealth as she liked without Sayrop's and Daniel's meddling. However, nothing in life is free; the expectation is that you will pay for it eventually.

Hussain Nadim Pasha had an Armenian secretary from Turkey, Sourain. It is he who is the instigator of Sarah's story. He had heard about Sarah's colossal wealth. It did not hurt that she was a beautiful seventeen-year-old with brown hair, a fair complexion, and bedroom eyes. She was also educated and charming. He devised a plan to marry Sarah through the backing and influence of Hussain. He also had access to her uncle and cousin, convincing them to advocate on his behalf. He solicited their help, promising to protect and cover up their discrepancies. He asked for her hand in marriage, but Sarah blatantly refused. Sourain was upset and decided to retaliate. With his ego hurt and calculating his vengeance, he convinced

Hussain that Sarah was a worthy catch. He knew it was unheard of for a woman such as Sarah, a devout Christian Armenian, to marry an Ottoman official who had been married several times, was a Muslim, and was considerably older than her. Sourain also reached out to Sayrop and Daniel, knowing they were resentful toward Sarah and would be more than happy to implement and support his vengeful plan.

Hussain Nadim Pasha

Hussain helped Sarah get control of her estate, and Sarah was grateful. But Sourain started to influence Hussain and slowly put his plan into motion, planting the seed and convincing him that Sarah was a worthy pursuit and love interest. The more Hussain thought about the idea, the more he warmed to it until he decided to ask for her hand in marriage. Hussain made a deal with Sayrop and Daniel. Hussain stated he would pardon Sayrop for the misuse of Sarah's funds, but only if they managed to convince Sarah to accept Hussain's marriage proposal.

The answer from Sarah, however, was a swift "No." But the more Sarah rejected, the more Hussain wanted her. A man like Hussain Nadim Pasha doesn't understand rejection. He became obsessed with her and wanted her at all costs. Through the help of Sayrop and Daniel, he made her life hell, even taking a sentimentally valued ring belonging to her late mother, with a small emerald surrounded by diamonds and smaller emeralds. She had to retrieve what belonged to her in person, accompanied by several people to support her, and put him to shame. That made him even more obsessed, and he spied on Sarah's every move and schemed ways to get her. Years later, a jeweler came to my father to sell the ring at his shop at the Baghdad hotel, but my father declined. My family doesn't buy something valuable from someone in need because we feel we are taking advantage of their misfortune. I feel strongly about it, and I have always honored this practice.

The incident caused an uproar and became a leading source of gossip in Iraqi social circles. It reached the media, causing media warfare between those against Hussain Nadim Pasha, who did not support the Ottoman occupation, and those allied with Hussain Nadim Pasha. It also meant that Hussain had to act fast and deal with Sarah to save face.

Word reached Sarah; Hussain was about to arrest her under fabricated pretenses, declaring she was insane, to have her at his mercy. It gave her no choice but to run to the German Ambassador. He was influential since the Ottomans had a strong relationship with Germany. Initially, Turkey wanted to stay neutral during World War I, but it soon became an ally of Germany. In addition, his residence was next door to her and her closest escape. She jumped over the boundary gate to the German Ambassador, and from there, she decided it was better to go to Abd al Rahman Al-Gillani, someone she respected and trusted, whose honesty and loyalty were displayed often. Most Iraqis held him in high regard. He was also a close friend of her late father's. The German Ambassador was Hussain's close friend, which unsettled her.

Hussain Nadim Pasha with his soldiers

Al-Gillani orchestrated her escape. He contacted the British on her behalf. The world was on the brink of war; the Germans were about to ally with the Turks—a dangerous combination. The British wanted to eliminate Hussain Nadim Pasha since his sympathies lay firmly with the Germans. A scandal would mean the end of Hussain's career and weaken Germany's hold. It also helped that Sarah's family had solid British ties. As I mentioned, Agha Khacheeq, Agha Minas, and Agha Mukail, her grandfather, had British nationality, as did her mother before she married. Sarah and those close to her decided she should travel to Bushehr in Iran and then go to London, England, to her mother's aunt. The best way to get to Bushehr was to use the British Lynch ships because Hussain had no jurisdiction when she stepped foot on them. Also mentioned previously was that Tang Khatoon's sister Ossana, Sarah's mother's aunt, married the sailor Stephen Lynch. Sarah was to embark on the Lynch cargo ship and sail to Bushehr. It was a safe and reliable way to take Sarah to safety.

Sarah had some additional assistance reaching the port. Even though Sarah was Armenian Orthodox, the "Rahibat" Presentation Sisters educated her generation, and she had close ties with the nuns, primarily through charity work. The Sisters disguised Sarah as a nun and smuggled her to the port so she could continue to Basra, along with an escort and a group of other nuns. Hussain heard about Sarah's clandestine departure and decided to intercept her journey. He sent his troops to stop her as he hurried to the port. On arrival at the port, Hussain and his troops frantically searched for Sarah. He came eye to eye with her but failed to recognize her since she was dressed as a nun, covered her face, and stood with a group of nuns. Sometimes, the best way to hide is to be blatant and obvious. Hussain, however, realized she would be using the Lynch ships, so he sent his troops to surveil and guard them.

Both pictures of Sarah Iskenderian during the 1910s

It put Sarah in a difficult position since it was almost impossible to embark on the ship without the troops noticing her. The nuns had an escort, and he was trying to find a solution to this problem. They could not get on. They knew a few steps into the vessel would lead to freedom. When he was looking around at the port, he noticed carpet sellers. He remembered Cleopatra, to see Caesar, was put and rolled into a carpet. He decided it was a chance worth taking. The escort rolled Sarah up inside the rug for her protection and safety. The escort paid a hefty sum for the seller to carry the carpet to the ship, which he did successfully. As soon as she embarked, she was safe on British soil.

Sarah is on her way to freedom.

Daniel Tatossian (Sarah's Husband)

Sarah stayed in Bushehr for almost a year before she continued to Europe. Sir Percy Cox looked after her, introduced to her by the Lynch side of the family, the new lieutenant colonel in Bushehr; the two forged a long friendship. He advocated and vouched for her mental well-being, declaring her sane and ensuring the Ottomans knew that, keeping her wealth safe from the clutches of Hussain Nadim Pasha and her uncle and cousin.

Hussain followed her to Bushehr and tried to see her several times, but she refused to see him. As a result of this scandal, Hussain Nadim Pasha was swiftly summoned back to Turkey in 1911. Sarah embarked on her journey from Bushehr to London, England, to her aunt's, and later to Paris, France. Sarah's destiny lay in Paris. There, she was to marry Daniel Tatossian, a businessman (not a doctor, as mentioned in some accounts). Daniel was the brother of Mariam Tatossian (my mother's paternal grandmother), who was married to Setrak (my mother's grandfather and Sarah's uncle). Daniel was related to Sarah through the marriage of relatives. He had two more brothers in Paris, Megrdeetch and Marcar, a doctor. Marcar married a Frenchwoman; the union produced no children. The rest of his siblings were in Baghdad.

Sarah was married in Paris. Daniel presented her with a Cartier wedding ring. My grandfather Vartan, his nephew through his mother's side and her cousin through his father, often stayed with his uncles in France for a long time. Later, when my grandfather married, he intended to move his family to France. He had even paid a down payment on a chateau, but this did not occur due to his untimely death in Jerusalem.

Sarah, on her wedding day with Daniel Tatossian.

Daniel Tatossian, now married to Sarah and living in Paris with his brothers, lived blissfully. A year after their marriage, Sarah gave birth to a boy; sadly, the infant boy died in Paris. After a few years, they returned to Baghdad to look after Sarah's vast wealth, especially since Hussain Nadim Pasha, having been sent back to Turkey, was no longer a threat, and the war was about to break out.

With the breakout of World War I and the dominance of the Ottoman Empire over Iraq, whose sympathies lay with Germany, the Armenians faced exile, and some were for a short period. The Ottoman representative after Hussain Nadim Pasha's expulsion, the new "Wali," welcomed back Armenians, revoking the decree after a month.

Daniel Iskenderian, Sarah's cousin, was one of the forty men exiled for a month. Her brother-in-law David was also expelled and died during the expulsion. There were also plans to banish a second group, including my mother's uncle, Minas, and her father, Vartan. It is unclear why Iraq deported those particular Armenians for a short period. Daniel and those exiled with him met Turkish Armenians who had escaped to Derzore (Syria). However, due to mounting pressure, the expelled from Iraq were welcomed back. One correspondence supporting the return of the deported Armenians is from the Hashimite House.

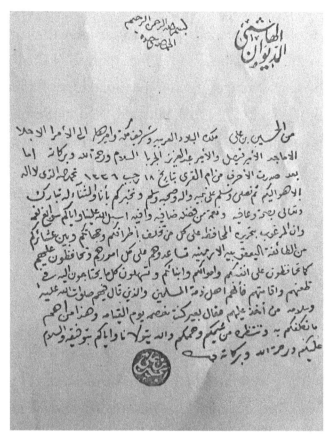

Letter from the Hashimite House (Husain Bin Ali) supporting the Armenians

In 1915, the Armenian genocide took place in Turkey. Daniel had substantial money in Derzore and took advantage of the survivors, buying their gold and gems for peanuts. Later, Daniel's daughter, Alice, greeted somebody wearing a ring made with one of those gems. Unbeknownst to her, someone took it from her finger. Another incident occurred while his daughter Melina was sleeping. A thief stole her earrings.

Different factors played a part in leading to the Armenian genocide. Armenians excelled in business through finance, so they started to influence politics, which didn't sit well with the Turks, especially Abdu'l-Hamid II. That Armenians were contributing positively and that they had been in Turkey for generations meant very little; they were taxed heavily and downgraded to being a separate group of the Ottoman society, which even labeled them as "millet," which led to the occupation of the Ottoman Bank in 1896. A mass exodus took place in 1915, but like everyone else, they were in denial that such an atrocity would occur. The Armenian priest in Baghdad knew this would happen, but no one believed such a thing would be possible on such a scale; the massacres started as early as the mid-1890s, and most thought they would be one-off incidents.

This incident took place only a few decades before the Jewish Holocaust. The survivors of this massacre started to flood into the Arab world and the neighboring countries. People shared stories about how they were tortured and burnt alive in pits; miraculously, a few survived, only to see their loved ones tortured and shot. These stories are compiled and should be shared more; as the Jews keep emphasizing, the Holocaust has to be remembered and engraved in history as an atrocity man mercilessly inflicted on his fellow man because it must never happen again. Sadly, man does not learn from past atrocities, nor is he remorseful.

The Armenian families in Baghdad, shocked at what they were hearing and, at the same time, being threatened with exile themselves, welcomed the survivors to their homes.

Over time, they helped them set up and establish roots in their new homeland.

In 1915, Sarah gave birth in Baghdad to her daughter, Sophie, whom she named after her mother. This happy occasion had a dark cloud over it since it was also the funeral of Ovaness Hovakimian, my mother's maternal grandfather. Edma followed Sophie in 1919, and in 1922, Percy followed, named after Sir Percy Cox, the first High Commissioner (1920-1923), his godfather, and his namesake.

Misery was to knock on Sarah's door again. She had just given birth to her son, who was barely forty days old when she lost her husband Daniel, who had a heart attack in Baghdad. The dates can vary, especially since those writing about Sarah took the dates from the church records. The church records, at the time, often record the date of baptism instead of birth. The dates I am sharing are the accurate ones. One of the titbits Sarah shared that she had heard from Sir Percy Cox was that Kuwait was part of Iraq. In the story, Sir Cox was among the dignitaries responsible for Iraq's destiny. He was the first High Commissioner in Baghdad and a strong ally of Ibn Saud. There were fears that he could potentially join forces with the Ottoman Empire. At that

Sir Percy Cox

time, Kuwait was a Basra district and an essential part of Iraq under the administrative rule of the Ottoman Empire due to its strategic position. In 1922, the fate of the border was in British hands. The British and Ibn Saud could not agree despite negotiating for a few days. Finally, Sir Percy Cox became impatient and summoned Sheikh Abdul-Aziz Ibn Saud, who was yet to become ruler of Saudi Arabia. Sir Cox explained the situation clearly and affirmed his standing that he would decide on the borders; taking a pen in hand, he marked a diamond on the map, declaring it the State of Kuwait.

Sarah, Sophie, Percy and Edma.

Sarah, Percy, Edma and Sophie

Sophie, Percy, and Edma.

Sarah's children (Edma, Percy and Sophie).

Again, Sarah was left alone but responsible for three children this time. She became overprotective of her children and began her ill-fated business ventures, mainly with the Makias and the Khuthairies. They convinced her to invest in agricultural machinery, and slowly, these failed ventures ate at her wealth. It did not help that she was a poor housekeeper and did not know the actual value of money. Sarah focused on her children and community for the next few years and tried to make sense of her heredity. She became a central figure in Iraq's British society. Sarah visited King Faisal's wife and later the mother of King Ghazi, Huzaima Bint Nasser. She mixed often with the elite of her generation in that part of the world, even with the likes of Gertrude Bell. She also donated "Camp Sarah" land to house Armenian refugees, which defined her and earned her name in Iraq's history.

Sarah Iskenderian Tatossian

Another story comes from when Sarah and her cousin Zabel (my mother's aunt) were neighbors in Karada. Their homes overlooked a public garden. One day, they received a ransom note stating that the kidnapping of one of their daughters would occur unless they paid a significant amount. The instructions were that Zabel's husband, Hyke, would deliver the money and place it at the bottom of a particular tree in the public garden. Hyke was terrified by his own shadow. This threat caused panic, forcing Sarah to call Iraq's Prime Minister Nuri al-Said. He instructed her to follow the instructions. Ten minutes before Hyke left his home with the ransom money, there was a blackout in the district. Terrified, he entered the park and placed the money under the designated tree. As soon as the kidnapper arrived, the lights came on, making the police who surrounded the garden visible, and they arrested him. It turns out it was the fruit monger across the street from them.

The next few years were the "golden" years. The social scene was at its best with parties, picnics, and travel. I have included some of the visits they made to Debouny and Annana at the time, even the house Sarah built in Baghdad. When I first saw the pictures, I could not help but notice the liberal fashion and the innocent, happy faces.

Sarah with friends in Debouny

Sarah with her Aunt Sophie (dressed in black next to her)

Picnic in Annana

Sarah next to the lions of Babylon

Annana

Picnic in Debouny

Debouny

Sarah and her husband in Debouny

"Gufa" Crossing from Annana to the Lions of Babylon

Annana

Annana

Annana

Debouny

Baghdad

Sarah's home in Baghdad

Sophie Tatossian

Edma Tatossian Romanovski

Percy Tatossian

Sarah Iskenderian Tatossian

Eventually, however, her investments in agricultural machinery caught up with her. The farmers wouldn't pay her what they owed her, claiming bad crops or blatantly ignoring her since she was a woman. The Makias further lent her money and charged her high interest until it accumulated so much that they forced her to use her home as collateral. This action enabled them to repossess her home, even turning off electricity and water to force her out, an act that degraded and humiliated her. It is insulting to hear a fabricated version of her story that she became a gambler and was an alcoholic, and that is why she lost her fortune; these are false accusations.

Edma (Sarah's daughter) has had a hip replacement.
Above is the last time the sisters Edma and Sophie were
together, in London, the U.K., visiting my mother.

Upon visiting my mother, Edma, Sophie shared her dismay at someone contacting her from Iraq's television studios to make her mother's life story into a series, something both she and her sister condemned. They came from a generation where you did not share details about your private life. They resented the phrase "Sarah Zanikina," meaning "Rich Sarah," when referring to their mother.

Sarah Iskenderian Tatossian

Sarah died in 1960; her wealth had diminished considerably, but she wasn't begging in the street. Her children buried her and not her maid or driver, another distorted version of her story. Her oldest daughter stayed a spinster and worked for the United Nations, sharing a home with Beatrice, their maid's daughter, paying her share and not freeloading on Beatrice. Percy married and had no children and died because of a senseless accident. He was an agent for some products and made his living based on commission. Edma lived in London, lived a conservative life, was debt-free, and died peacefully in 1997, and it is due to her that I have those pictures and information.

Sarah's bankruptcy left her and her children scarred and distrustful. Once she declared bankruptcy, my grandmother agreed to state that Sarah owed her money, thus confiscating Sarah's shares of Annana (Annana was divided into shares that the descendants inherited). Once things calmed down, my grandmother returned the claims to her. Her daughter never failed to mention this, and how grateful she was, so she trusted my mother implicitly.

Sarah Iskenderian Tatossian

Money goes and comes. You must respect it and know how to maintain its value when it comes. Unfortunately, no one taught Sarah the responsibility or worth of money, and crimes within the family are challenging to persecute with in-depth sentiments attached.

I want to touch on Regina Iskenderian, née Mekrdjian. I want to mention her to show the connection between her and Sarah. Sarah and Regina are renowned Armenian women from that era in Iraq. Regina married Sarah's cousin Daniel (Yes, the Daniel that caused Sarah so much anguish), who was older than her by seventeen years. She was also the niece of Daniel Tatossian, Sarah's husband.

Regina had two daughters who died in adulthood. Their unions produced no children. Her wealth came from Daniel, which came from Sarah, which is ironic. Regina is probably best remembered for her considerable contributions to the community, especially for establishing the "Old People's Home." One of the things Sarah used to say was, "May God wipe them off the face of the earth." Her wish became a reality since no descendants are alive today.

Daniel, Sarah's cousin and Regina's husband, was responsible for another scandal. I mentioned earlier that Sarah's mother and two sisters stole Agha Mukail's deeds so their brother did not inherit anything. Sarah's aunts had moved to Istanbul when they got married. When they died, their husbands wanted to sell everything they owned in Baghdad, so they gave power of attorney to Vartan, my maternal grandfather, and his brother Minas, Setrak's sons. The law states you cannot record the piece of land in your name if you serve as the power of attorney. They wanted to buy properties to keep them in the family. They decided to record the land in Daniel's name and send the money to their husbands in Istanbul. However, Daniel chose to keep the property, which caused the family to fall out. I have no idea why and what possessed them to go about this process in this way since it is clear how dishonest Daniel was due to what he did to Sarah.

Regina often visited Vartan's sister, Aroos, since they were cousins. Whenever my grandfather Vartan called on his sister, and Regina was there, he used to sit outside the front door and tell his sister to "kick that raven out" in the most audible voice. They went to court for years, but they never got anything. At some point, Daniel bribed the government official with emeralds, ones he had purchased cheaply during his temporary deportation to Derzone (Syria).

There is a story where Regina had some guests, and they witnessed that citrus fruit was brought to her from her orchards. The maid asked her what to do with it since there was so much. Regina instructed her to throw them into the river. The guest asked if they could take it; Regina said throwing it into the river was better. That way, there would not be any issues. It shows you that Regina was a complex woman, and probably, with her late husband's damaging actions, she tried to put people at a distance.

Regina later moved to Lebanon due to her daughter's illness. Her daughter's husband worked in the American Embassy in the 1950s. It was a time of chaos, and many did leave Baghdad.

At that time, one of the greatest scandals in Armenian society was Skender Tatossian's mother's murder. Skender, the cousin of Sarah's children, was my grandfather, Vartan's maternal cousin, and my uncle Edmond's godfather. In a rage, he stabbed his mother my maternal grandmother's aunt) forty times. Someone else may have committed the crime, causing added controversy. He was put in an asylum in Lebanon for over twenty years and released. On his release, Sophie, Sarah's daughter, took him in until his death.

That is not the only murder that took place in the Armenian community. There was the murder of Vahan, the priest, and his wife. A man asked for his daughter's hand in marriage. Vahan rightly said, "You have nothing; go and make something of yourself, and then come and marry my daughter." The suitor shot Vahan, his wife, and himself in a rage.

Sarah did leave a fantastic legacy and lived a life that came out of a novel. It saddens me that she was taken advantage of, especially by her family. In life, trusting people is inevitable; the problem is few are worthy. As a woman like Sarah in Baghdad, I felt alone and bewildered. My lifeline did not come from my family but from strangers—our lawyers were rare gems in a coal mine. In our case, there was forgery, lies, and backstabbing; one only helped you if they got their pound of flesh, which could change in a fraction of a second if the other side offered more. I understand and feel for Sarah and her predicament. My heart goes out to her.

# Chapter 7

## Skender Stephan and His Family

In this chapter, I will discuss Skender Stephan, my paternal grandfather. I will also discuss his immediate family and that of his wife, Asgheek. Skender was born in Baghdad, Iraq, in 1895 and died in Geneva, Switzerland, in 1991. He left us a remarkable legacy that we are proud of and hope to pass on to our children. He was a social man who worked hard and accomplished a

Skender Stephan

great deal. I didn't grow up in Baghdad, but I hear nothing but respect and admiration whenever I meet someone, and they realize I am his granddaughter.

However, sometimes reference is made to his alleged indiscretions. I find it in poor taste for people who barely know me and have never met him to feel a need to mention this to me immediately. Like many great men, he was complex, with many tragedies in his life that marred him. Out of his grandchildren, the ones who knew him best were my two cousins from my aunt's side and myself since we grew up close to him. My father, John, is his eldest living son.

Every summer, we would visit him in the south of France, and every winter break, we would see him in Geneva, Switzerland, to be with him. One noticeable thing about my Grandfather was that he had a presence and loved people who loved him back. He had strong communication skills, great charm, and always had a twinkle in his eye. He worked hard and played harder. Despite all his success, he taught us to be humble and grateful. A proverb states, "Do not mix business with pleasure." My grandfather's success, however, was because he mixed business with pleasure.

Grandfather Skender's passport states he was born in 1895, but according to the church records, he was born in 1901. His brother Ohan was born in 1901. At that time, as previously mentioned, the church sometimes recorded the baptism date, not birth. His second brother is Ohan, followed by Leon, Armina, Aram, and Victoria. He was the eldest of six children with a very domineering mother. Stephan, his father, was a prominent figure in the Medan district. His family goes back as far as 1639, and a stream of his ancestry, before 1639, had lived in Basra. Stephan Markar Davitian was secretary for the Ministry of Exterior in Baghdad. His uncle was Baghdassar Davitian, who had been sent to study in Turkey and was ordained a priest, changing his name to Mesorb Davitian and was responsible for the Sourp Tarkmanechatz Varjarian (School of Holy Translators) and served the community as a priest. Stephan married a woman considerably younger than himself, Deroohy.

Deroohy always made my grandfather feel responsible for his siblings, especially since her husband died when most of her children were young. The spelling of the names varies. For example, Stephan and Stepan are the same person. It depends on who and where you have seen the translated name and relies heavily on the translator's ability and command of the language at the time, who is translating them from either Armenian or Arabic. I applied what is the most common. The church registers some family members under other names, specifically Armenian ones, including mine. An example is my father's cousin, Margos, who is named Margos in the church, but the family knows him as Farid.

Grandfather Skender came from a humble beginning, especially since he had lost his father at a young age, forcing him to grow up fast and making him the head of the family. He became a head that everyone respected. He stood by his siblings and watched their backs. In turn, they went to him for guidance and wisdom. He was a very generous man. Grandfather's brother Ohan married his cousin Eugene Yeghiayan, which caused Deroohy to be unhappy, as she saw Eugene as unsuitable despite the fact she was her niece. Ohan went with a gun and declared that he would kill himself unless allowed to marry Eugene. My grandfather supported his decision and moved him to Numania. Eugene and Uncle Ohan had Jalal, Helal, Dalia, and the twins Kamal and Jamal.

Eugene loved music and was responsible for the church choir. Grandfather set up Armina and Victoria in a home and registered it in their name in case they did not marry to secure their future. Armina married Arsen Iskenderian later in adulthood and had two sons, Farid (Margos) and Edmond.

Grandfather Skender's brother Leon married an English lady named Delores and had two children, David and Davina, who resided in the U.K. Grandfather's brother, Aram, worked in the distillery and built a house in Bataween, which he rented while he lived with his family.

My grandfather was a family man who would have been astonished to see brothers stab each other in the back and deceive each other. In our case, the following generation seemed to excuse themselves from stealing from each other, even in one instance, standing by a stranger who had deceived, forged documents, broken the law, and disrespected us, even by executing one of us (a story alluded to earlier and still to come).

When my grandmother married my grandfather, they lived moderately, but my grandfather was ambitious, hard-working, loved people, was a master at networking, and knew how to ingratiate himself. They were relatively happy, but what broke them was their loss of five children. Their oldest child, George, died as a teenager from diphtheria, followed by four more infants; one girl was named Hilda, and one boy was named Kevork (born in 1921). Some died from childhood diseases. The death of their children was a taboo subject, never to be brought up before my grandparents.

My grandfather spent every waking minute of his day working to escape his grief and manage his vast responsibilities. After the death of his oldest son, he was never the same. He started by selling raw agricultural materials such as wheat and corn. Then, he became an agent for Case Agricultural Equipment. He sold the equipment to the farmers in Numania and Kut and formed lifelong friendships with the locals, who always had a special place in his heart. He changed our family surname from "Markarian," previously "Davitian," a surname used by his grandfather, Markar, to "Stephan," his father's name. He did so because his business associates found it difficult to pronounce "Markarian," and it was easier to use "Stephan."

Then, he progressed to being an agent to sell oil; Abdul Kadir Pasha al Khuthairi was responsible for giving him this opportunity. His business ventures led to the factory of cotton seeds. The factory made different kinds of soap. One soap bar named after my Aunt Aida did well; unfortunately, another named after my father's cousin Dalia did not do so well.

The nationalization of the factory industry around 1963/1964 destroyed another part of my grandfather. However, he also had his fingers in many pots, including having shares in a distillery managed by his brother Aram for a time. However, with indirect outside threats about letting the authorities know we lived abroad, he thought it was a better idea to sell them. My grandfather's wisdom was exemplary. He taught us never to show what accomplishments we strived towards or materialistically what we have and, most importantly, to stay under the radar and to stand by each other. The more you work hard and achieve, the more resentful and jealous people are, leading them to act vengefully.

Cinema Khayam

Hotel Khayam

The era of Omar Khayyam, a Persian poet, astronomer, mathematician, and philosopher in the eleventh century, appealed to my grandfather, especially his artistic use of colors, Persian style, and the designs used in his work. He decided to build the Khayam Cinema, authentically refurbishing it and expanding it with the opening of Hotel Khayam in 1956. He hired an entire European staff, with the first hire being Hans Maschek, an Austrian hotel manager.

## New Cinema for Baghdad

A remarkable new cinema in the South Gate quarter of Baghdad. Reputed to be the most up to date in the Middle East, this cinema was recently completed at a cost of about £300,000. Fully air-conditioned, the theatre has 1,500 seats in stalls and balcony, is equipped with the most modern projection apparatus yet made, and has a screen 50 feet wide. Marble imported from Italy has been used lavishly, while sliding red-plush seats, imported from the United States, and fitted pile carpets, make it one of the most comfortable and luxurious cinemas in the world. Outstanding features are, however, giant murals depicting characters from Omar Khayyam, and the ceiling, designed to represent a sky of twinkling stars.

**The Passing Scene**—continued

*Photography by Jack Percival*
*Baghdad Photographic Unit*

Executed in traditional Persian style by the Italian painter, Enrice Brandoni, the murals give a startling effect when bathed in ultra-violet light. Special equipment was installed to distribute sound evenly throughout the auditorium : and the ceiling and walls were treated by a French engineer, Marcel Barthelemy, to guarantee absorption of echo. For the convenience of patrons, the large foyer with its concealed lighting, varnished wood-work, huge mirrors and polished marble, contains not only a bar but also an unusual type of automatic slot machine for dispensing a wide variety of soft drinks—ranging from hot chocolate to iced orangeade.

A French interior decorator, Lucien Polya, was responsible for the cinema's striking interior effects : and construction of the building was supervised by L. Boghossian.

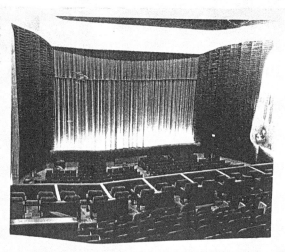

42

Article on Khayam Cinema and Hotel

150

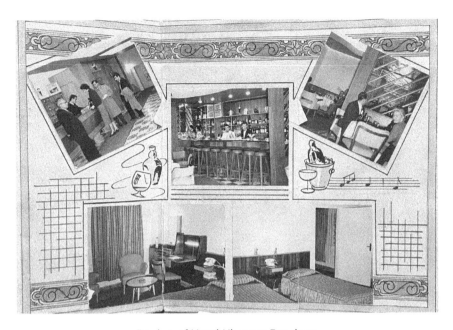

Design of Hotel Khayam Brochure

Helga Werner

The next hire was a German housekeeper, Helga Werner. Austrians made up the majority of the staff. The receptionist convinced everyone to go on strike, demanding more pay. This action upset my grandfather, who let go of most of them. He replaced them with a newly recruited Lebanese staff, but not managers.

Our home in Masbah

After my parents married, they resided at the hotel until they moved to their new home in Masbah. Around that time, Afifa Skender lived at the hotel. Over the years, she forged a close relationship between herself and my family. She may have had a relationship with my grandfather, but she was also a close family friend who provided him with a vast Baghdad network of powerful men. My grandfather, however, never neglected his wife and provided her with a life of luxury. The name of the man who discovered Afifa was Iskandar, and she adopted it as her surname. We believe her heritage was partially Greek and not Armenian.

My grandfather was also involved in trade delegations to the United States on behalf of Iraq. He was a prominent figure in Iraq's finance world. Among his friends were ministers and dignitaries. He received two medals; one was for participating in a delegation, and the other was due to his monetary donations. In 1958, my grandfather felt unsafe in Baghdad. He, a friend, Nigel al Khuthairi, and Afifa Skender were the first to leave Baghdad. At first, he went to Beirut, Lebanon, staying at the St. George Hotel, and then settled between Geneva, Switzerland, and Nice in the south of France. My grandmother left with him temporarily but missed her family and returned to Baghdad to be close to her children, family, and friends.

Days started to become weeks, and my grandfather decided to hire a housekeeper. He called on the former housekeeper of Hotel Khayam, Helga Werner, to look after his household. One memory I have of my paternal grandmother was that she used to have a display of framed pictures of the family. Every time I visited her, I checked to see who had fallen out of grace—she would remove the photos of those she was upset with. If she had removed your photographs, you would have fallen out of favor with her. Although he died in Geneva, my grandfather never thought he belonged in Europe, and his heart and soul belonged to Baghdad. It was a love that never died. There was a date tree, the Al Asreq (blue) kind, at my grandmother's house, and because of the tree, the house floorplan was all wrong. An indent in the floor plan, like a closed narrow corridor outside, cut into the center of the house just because of the tree and how the sun hit it. A window was looking out, and you could see the boundary wall a few meters behind the tree. We would bring a bag of dates from that tree whenever we visited him from Baghdad. He used to treasure it, and each morning, he would indulge in a few dates and sit and reminisce about his birthplace.

The picture represents an Iraqi delegate to the United States in 1944. From the left: Abdulhadi Al Chalabi, Hafeth Al Qathi, Nouri Fatah Basha, and Kthuri Shukur. Standing: Meer Basri, on the right, and Skender Stephan.

Armenian Gathering sometime between 1938 and 1940. Sitting from right: Skender Stephan , Khosrov Kuyemjian, Garabet Melkonian. Standing from right: Levon Shahoian, Sarkis Zulemian, Nishan Hagopian, Israel Zokian

Wedding of John Stephan and Edma Minas 1965

Another notable story of my grandfather's life in Baghdad is how he got involved with V.I.P.s who were visiting, such as during the coronation of King Faisal II when he came of age in 1953. Many dignitaries from all over the world were to attend his coronation. Baghdad could not house so many V.I.Ps at the time since it did not have the facilities. The answer to this question was to use Baghdad's renowned houses temporarily. Thus, my grandfather's house was designated to house the American delegate. The homeowners could stay in their residences but only utilize a small section. On the departure of the dignitaries, the United States delegate gave my grandfather a gift as a gesture of appreciation. It was a framed photograph of the diplomat and his wife. On his guest's departure, my grandfather's friend, Sayed Sulaiman Sheikh Doud, a renowned lawyer who housed the representatives from Bahrain, was given a pearl necklace.

From L. to R.: Nimette Minas, Berj Kantarjian, Shereen Al Haidery, The bride Edma Minas, Yasmeen Al Haidery, Aida Stephan and Karnig Kantarjian

Najwa Fouad at my parent's wedding

Saleema Murad at my parent's wedding

Afifa Iskender at my parent's wedding

Celebrations were important to my grandfather, Skender, and other family members. The years leading up to my parents' wedding were unstable, especially with the revolution in 1958. Leon, my grandfather's brother, died, which meant a morning period for his brother had to be respected. It reminds me of the pandemic and how it felt when the restrictions ended. Weddings and celebrations were back on course. With the revolution and the curfews in the country over, the Iraqi people had felt confined, and finally, in 1965, it was time to live again, and my parents decided to get married then. Since it was the first big event in the family, my grandfather decided it would be a monumental wedding to celebrate a hopeful era. It isn't nice to look at the pictures and think of one of the most lavish parties we have held; there have been many that I couldn't attend.

My grandfather would visit Baghdad periodically; during that time, he would catch up with family and friends, a time he cherished. My grandfather had access to the world, and see it he did, but his eyes would light up upon his return to Baghdad.

On one occasion, my grandfather left Baghdad for Geneva via Beirut. On one of his trips, he was seated next to someone famous. We asked him who he was sitting next to on his arrival in Geneva. He said, "A delightful woman. Her name was Greta Garbo." Greta Garbo made no sense to us since no one heard that she was in Baghdad. We inquired further and discovered that it was Sabah, a Lebanese singer. My grandfather treated everyone the same way. The essential trait of a human being is humility.

My grandfather's Name Day is the social calendar's biggest party of the year. Iraq's best artists sang for the occasion, including Nathem al Ghazali, Salima Murad, Saadoun Jaber, and Afifa Skender. In one instance, an invitation is extended to a particular artist to perform at the height of his career; as he took a break, he relaxed sitting on the sofa, eating pistachios and putting the shells between the cracks. The maid took an ashtray for him. He told her it was easier to put it between the cracks of the sofa. It was surreal the following day to say what happened to my friends.

In Geneva, my grandfather opened a hotel, "Rivoli," and bought property all over Switzerland and France but decided to live a simple life at that stage. He rented his flat and did not live in one of his properties. His apartment was small and basic, but his bedroom was full of antiques, a haven. When I visited him, he would spoil me and give me substantial pocket money to buy whatever I wanted and bus tickets. Taking taxis back was not allowed; only travel by bus and walking was acceptable.

He called some of the most influential men of his time from Iraq and Iran friends, and they would visit him from time to time to play backgammon. He would walk to a nearby café and meet his friends, all men from his era, and they would sit and talk about the glory days, and each would pay for his coffee. The message is simple: live humbly and enjoy luxuries for yourself; don't show off. Be selective with your friends and look for essential traits such as loyalty and integrity. Never use your friends and stand by them in their time of need. Your actions define the person you are. Before my grandfather passed away, he reminded my father to hand over land in Numania. It belonged to some of his friends, although the title was under his name. It shows that you have integrity, and honesty is what defines you. In the summers, he moved to his flat in Nice in the south of France. The French Riviera was always fun, and I have many happy memories there.

The older my grandfather got, the more dependent he became on his housekeeper, Helga Werner. He married her, and she took good care of him, living to be 96 years old. He died in 1991 in Geneva, Switzerland.

Stephan Markarian, as he was known then

Stephan (Markarian) (Davitian) with his wife
Deroohy and his sons Skender and Ohan

Stephan (Markarian) (Davitian) and Deroohy Der Yeghiayan 1898

Deroohy and her husband, Stephan, are sitting in the picture. On
the left. Standing behind them are Ama Noush, her brother(they
were orphans whose aunt is Deroohy), and, to the right, Ohan.
L to R, Armina, Aram, and Victoria on the ground.

L to R: Skender, Leon, and Ohan

In addition to my grandfather, other members of this side of my family also have notable stories about them. Grandfather's mother, Deroohy, was a stubborn, strong woman. Along with her parents, Der Avedees (born in 1839) and Martha (who changed her name from Nazli Kharabo (Khazmo)), and brothers and sisters, she came to Baghdad through Sghert [Siirt] in Turkey and Mosul. She had nine siblings: Gohar (born in Siirt), Hripsime (born in Mosul), Hovakim (born in Mosul), Michael (born in Mosul), Anna (born in Siirt), Deroohy (born in Mosul), and Mariam (born in Mosul). One confusion I had was that they had another Hovakim and Deroohy in the family (so confusing to use the same names repeatedly), and Gabriel all died in infancy. Some were born in Siirt and some in Mosul. Der Avedees was a priest and seemed to have moved constantly between Mosul and Siirt until finally settling in Baghdad. Hovakim, his son, worked in trade, and two of his sons, Dikran and Setrak, worked with him. They were known as "Papas Oglum" in Turkish, meaning sons of priests, and that led them to change their surnames to Papazian. I also found it interesting that the Armenians living in Mosul (north of Iraq) adopted Arabic names in the mid-1800s. That could be because they wanted to blend in, especially with the hostility brewing in Turkey and the treatment of Armenians.

One of Deroohy's brothers and the fourth child was Zaven I Der Yeghiayan (his previous name was Michael). Zaven was born in Mosul in 1868 and educated at the Armash Seminary in Turkey. Upon consecration to a priest, he changed his name from Michael to Zaven. He then became a Bishop in Diyarbakir. He was ordained in 1913, at the age of forty-five, and served as Constantinople's Armenian Patriarch until 1922. In 1916, due to the Armenian genocide, he was exiled to Baghdad. In 1919, he returned to Istanbul, but In 1922, he had to leave Istanbul as a "persona non grata." [13]After a detour via Syria, Mosul, and Baghdad in 1926, he left for Cyprus to become the director plenipotentiary of the Melkonian Institute. His family had sent many boys to Istanbul for academic studies at his expense, but not my grandfather since he had to take care of the family.

---

13  "Armenian Patriarchate of Constantinople." New Articles RSS, International Encyclopedia of World War I, 18 May 2020, encyclopedia.1914-1918-online.net/article/armenian_patriarchate _of_constantinople.

Deroohy Der Yeghiayan

Zaven I Der Yeghiayan

When Grandfather Skender moved out to build his own family, he bought a home for his sisters and also to house his mother. Deroohy lived with her daughters, Armina and Victoria, and one of her sons, Aram, who remained unmarried. She was close to her daughter Armina and her family. She had a firm hold on my grandfather, psychologically manipulating him into being responsible for the whole family, even in adulthood. The strong family resemblance between Deroohy and Zaven I Der Yeghiayan is evident.

Zaven finally ended up in Baghdad, where he wrote his memoirs, *My Patriarchal Memoirs*,[14] which gives insight into attempts by the patriarch himself to stop the atrocities inflicted on his people in Turkey. The Turks, however, had a plan; I don't think anything would have swayed them. His most significant achievement, other than helping a minority of the Armenian people flee, was to try to inform the rest of the world of what was taking place in Turkey.

Hovakim and his wife Antaram, his daughter Eugene,
Zaven I Der Yeghiayan and his other daughter Eliz

---

14    *My Patriarchal Memoirs* by Zaven Der Yeghiayan can be found at Academia.edu: https://www.academia.edu/42653798/Zaven_Der_Yeghiayan_My_Patriarchal_Memoirs

Zaven later bought a house in Baghdad, in the Bataween district, and lived there until he died in 1947. He retreated there to write his memoirs. He later had throat surgery and lost his voice. His burial place is in Jerusalem, as he had requested. The genocide left him deeply scarred and bewildered. His family had been priests for thirteen generations.

Skender married my grandmother, Asgheek, who came from a wealthy family. Asgheek's mother's family settled in the north, in Mosul, for a time. Her mother Eliza's family, on their arrival there, converted to Protestant Christians due to missionaries. Her father, Yousef Saati Abrahamian, was a respected watchmaker and fixed and sold watches. He also imported the Zenith brand and traveled to Europe and Japan for trade. He manufactured watches with his name embedded in them. There is a street named after him in Baghdad.

Skender Stephan and Asgheek Abrahamian

Skender Stephan is with his bride Asgheek Abrahamian. The bridesmaids are Armina and Victoria Stephan. 1924

Yousef al Saati (Abrahamian) 1936

There was significant opposition to my grandmother marrying my grandfather, especially since she is part protestant. Asgheek's sister, Victoria's engagement ended due to this kind of opposition based on religious differences, even after she had ordered her dowry and wedding gown from Paris. The same fate fell on their sister, Mari. She was never married. Mari went to live in Australia and later in the United States. They had three brothers, Edward, Samuel, and Hagop, an optometrist. Their descendants now live in the United States.

The only one to survive out of my grandfather and grandmother's first five children was my Aunt Aida, born in 1928. My grandmother was desperate for a son. She heard an old wives' tale from the wife of Kamal Kuthairi. The folktale states that she should adopt a wolf cub on the birth of a son. Kamal's wife did the same and named her son "Theeb," who later changed his name to Muthafer and survived. My grandmother gave birth to my father, John, in 1937 and adopted a wolf cub. She used to swear that whenever my father was sick, she would go to the cub and plead with him for my father to get better. She used to say the wolf would get sick, and my father would get better. My father still has a pendant of the wolf's tooth.

From the left, Eliza (mother), Yousef al Saati Abrahamian, and Asgheek are sitting. The little girl on the left is standing Mari, and Victoria is standing to the right. At the back, L to R: Samuel and Hagop

Victoria was my father's maternal aunt, a colorful, eccentric character. My grandmother Asgheek was fair-skinned and had light brown hair and green eyes. Her sister Mari was blond, blue-eyed, and fair-skinned. Victoria was tanned, had a mop of untamed black hair, and had very dark eyes that pierced through you. Her sense of humor was dry, and her explanation for her coloring was that her mother was pregnant during the entrance of the Indian/Nepalese Gurkhas in Iraq. Her mother's cravings during her pregnancy somehow affected her baby's complexion.

Victoria always had the most bizarre stories to share. She used to work at a bank and was very suspicious of everyone, yet she was also gullible and would believe anything. She would frequently disappear for months. The reasons would be either her being upset about something we are unaware of or her having returned from a holiday and sharing her adventures of traveling abroad. The places she visited were not as accessible as they are now, and travel to those places rarely took place then. She mainly targeted East European countries or the Far East. She would come back with the most elaborate jewelry made from semi-precious stones.

Victoria had a habit of buying Iraqi government bonds and was so suspicious of everyone that she hid them in the structure of her home. On one occasion, she complained that the mice had eaten them! In one instance, my uncle needed confirmation from someone at the bank who knew him that he was who he claimed to be. He asked that she verify who he was since she worked there. The responsibility involved in doing so was too great for her.

In another instance, my uncle bought a parrot from his friend. Little known to him, the parrot had a foul vocabulary. One afternoon, she visited my uncle and aunt, and as Victoria waited for my aunt in the living room, the parrot, a master at mimicking voices, decided to use my cousin's voice and share profanities with her. She was appalled and upset, and she accused my cousin of being rude to her. After that incident, she did not visit my uncle for a while.

As she grew older, she was found unconscious and admitted to the Armenian Old People's Home. Our church's priest, the deacon's son Der Nareek, arranged for the church to take her property. At the Old People's Home, she appeared trauma-tized. She seemed pressured into revealing where she hid her jewelry, coins, and bonds. After clearing her ransacked home, they found empty holes under the fridge and walls.

My parents knew how to throw a party. Preparations would start weeks before the big event. My mother and father would discuss the menu extensively. My mother is a gourmet cook who loves a challenge and always comes up on top, impress-ing the most demanding palate. My grandfather's and, later, my parents' parties were legendary, with the most fantastic cuisine, entertainment, and company. They were carefully orchestrated with detailed precision to offer the best available.

My father has always been artistic and loved to entertain. His vocation in life has always been designing. He secured an internship in Paris but could not fulfill his dream. He always tried to push my children toward something creative, but we all excelled in anything but art. His father encouraged him to pursue business, and he attended the London School of Economics. He later also gained a degree in Hotel Management from Glion, Switzerland.

My father remained in Baghdad and worked to look after my grandfather's legacy. My parents were the golden couple—my father, who had charisma and wit, and my mother, who oozed sophistication. In the summers, we went to Europe for four months and then returned to Baghdad to resume our lives.

As I mentioned, my father's vocation in life was not business but art. He Loved paintings, music, fashion, and entertainment.

He was always an edgy dresser, which conflicted with my mother's and my conservative classical fashion sense. At my aunt's engagement, I remember he wore a silver top and a purple suit for her wedding. It was the 70s, after all! He went on strict diets and shopped at Europe's most renowned boutiques and stores. In one instance, he bought a labeled tuxedo from Harrod's of London—a piece of exquisite design and beautiful craftsmanship. In Baghdad, there was an Armenian tailor, Harout. The community very well respected Harout's reputation as a tailor, and he was in high demand; his clientele was the elite of Baghdad. Harout's prime was at the time of the rise of Saddam Hussein; he, too, had become a client. Harout came to my father and asked him if he had a tuxedo. My father showed him the one he had just bought, and Harout begged my father to give it to him. My father is 5'9" and has more of a petite build; this was during his skinniest phase. Saddam was over 6' and "bigger built," with broad shoulders and much longer legs, which added to his charisma and presence. It always intrigued us how Harout adjusted the tuxedo to fit Saddam.

My father visited Baghdad in the 1980s. At the airport customs, they took your passports, stamped them, and returned them to you. They told my father the head wanted to see him. You go through many emotions when you are told such a thing in a country under dictatorship. My father was no different. After what seemed like a lifetime (it was an hour), my father walked through a long corridor to a large office. A military man greeted him, sat him down, and told him he had heard many good things from those close to him about his father and wanted to meet his son.

I remember once visiting Baghdad during the Christmas holidays. On leaving Baghdad, customs stopped us. The customs officer asked me where I went to school. I replied in English with a very upper-class accent. He stared at me, puzzled. Then, he turned to my father and said, "Travel for all students during the academic year is prohibited; she cannot leave." My father didn't know what to do or say. He stood there silently reflecting and thinking to himself, gesturing his hands in a circular motion as he reminisced, asking himself what to do. The man felt his motions meant I was crazy; at that point, he stamped my passport and wished me a speedy recovery.

Another story is of when my uncle was the only one in Baghdad. One night, he received a phone call informing him that he and his family would go to an auditorium the next day to meet a bus. The caller did not share the reason. The next day, my uncle decided to wear his best suit regardless. He, his wife, and his son went to the auditorium, and a bus with blacked-out windows picked them up. It took them to an undisclosed destination, and it was there that Saddam presented my uncle with a medal for my grandfather for his donations. Wherever we settled, one rule was not to go near politics or share our political views, which contradicts human nature since everyone has an opinion. Like many others, the regime pressured and coerced us into offering a gift to the "government." You were either with or against them; neutrality was not an option. We did so to be left alone and sublimate into society.

During Saddam's reign of terror, there was no loyalty between friends or relatives. Mothers, fathers, sons, daughters, and siblings were encouraged to report each other should they stand against the regime; this left mistrust and each man to fend for himself. The family unit was left distorted, which significantly impacted psychological well-being. It allowed Saddam to control and influence the Iraqi people and planted the seed of disloyalty and mistrust towards each other. Judging by the situation now, it stripped people of any freedoms and kept them safe from each other.

On a short visit to Baghdad in the late 1980s, I saw Saddam's picture on the piano amongst family photographs and wondered whether we were related or close friends. Then I noticed his picture displayed at every home. The names of fathers and grandfathers identified people; abolishing surnames to strip people of their identity and avoiding distinguishing the tribes became a common practice. People would silently curse the regime yet simultaneously verbally say positive things or speak in code in case someone was eavesdropping.

The worst of the two eras, Saddam's period and post-era, is what defines the Iraqi people now, sadly. Corruption and minimal ethics, non-accountability, and irresponsibility are part of the system now. I don't want to generalize since many Iraqis still have principles, and throughout my ordeal, they have been instrumental in my quest for the truth. However, I wonder if ethics, loyalty, and integrity will someday identify us again. Each Iraqi is accountable; where do we start to remedy this?

As I mentioned, my grandfather left us a legacy to be proud of. However, recent events did tarnish that. Our "representative" actions caused us the most damage inflicted by him acting on our family name's behalf, something we take great pride in and live incredibly ethically for the sake of. My late uncle recommended him, even going so far as to advocate for him, although we voiced our concerns. It did not help that we no longer lived in Iraq, and the impact of the fall of Iraq in 2003 tied our hands. It was a time of uncertainty and confusion. He is also my cousin Nazar's killer, Ayad Tareq Ahmed Al Mashaykhi, who exploited us. He forged power of attorneys, even supposedly from embassies. He took a massive loan under my father's name without his knowledge, lying and constantly stealing, resurrecting my deceased aunt from the dead, and fabricating a vacuum of fear and emotional distress. He is a graduate of Saddam's secret service, and that should indicate the person he is.

He built a tourist empire, Beyond Borders, with ethical issues in the Middle East. He manages Syria and Egypt Air in Baghdad, someone with no integrity. He used his position to manipulate others and serve his needs, even when taken in for questioning regarding his involvement in the killing in Baghdad of Qasem Soleimani, a prominent Iranian general, which sends shudders down my spine; he has loyalty towards no one. He disregarded and disrespected us and does not represent my family, nor should he act on our behalf. My cousin Farid cut off all ties with us and remained his partner; Ayad remained his representative in Baghdad, even while we were going through a court case and needed his guidance. I have kept a comprehensive documented account of this and will write about our ordeal in the future, but I am not ready at the moment; the hurt and betrayal run too deep.

Until his death, my grandfather remained the son of Baghdad. Though some members of my family turned their backs on the values Grandfather Skender represented, others, like my father, continued to uphold those values. How do you turn back time and remind the new generation that we have integrity, loyalty, ethics, pride, and care about each other? Our words and actions are what speak volumes about us.

# Chapter 8

## Guards and Thieves of Baghdad

In this chapter, I would like to focus on our guards, especially since they were with us most of the time. Their ancestors were former thieves who raided Baghdad but soon became guards and have the most colorful, entertaining stories.

When Agha Mukail, my great-great-grandfather, and his father, Agha Minas, immigrated to Baghdad, they bought a seven-million-square farm plot. There were agricultural farmers along the river from Masbah to Muasker al Rasheed. It was a heaven of various fruits, especially citrus fruit, which was later a passion of my grandfather, Vartan, when he eventually inherited the land. There were tribes from Mahweel in Hillah who used to venture by boat, cross the river, and steal from the orchards. He got sick of this and talked with the tribe's head. In their discussion, Agha Mukail decided to throw a radical idea. Agha Mukail asked the tribe's leader to provide him with men to guard the orchards. This deal started a relationship that lasted for three generations.

The guards were highly skilled and closely watched everything within the property, especially since they were professional robbers simultaneously. The men who served us were the most loyal, protective, and loving men we had encountered. They guarded us and cared about us like we were their own family. Each member of the family had a guard from the tribe. Adai served Vartan, my grandfather. I remember him having white hair with piercing eyes and being fiercely loyal to my grandmother, always calling her "Khatoon" as a form of respect. During World War II, because my grandfather was British, he and his wife and son had to reside in the British Embassy to guarantee their safety. My mother, aunt, and maternal grandmother stayed at the house protected by the tribe.

The hidden car during WWII

In my grandfather's absence, Adai hid his car since it was a hot commodity, especially the tires since it was wartime. As the attackers knew it was an allied home, they severely beat Adai and tried to force him to reveal the car's location, but Adai refused.

Grandfather Vartan had traveled to Paris during the outbreak of World War II. He had no option but to flee on the Orient Express. Going to Jerusalem, he sadly died of a heart attack, his last resting place. On hearing the news, Adai was inconsolable. My mother has vivid memories of him hitting himself over his head. He had lost his best friend and "brother."

When my mother was five, she was diagnosed with diphtheria. Because she had an infectious disease, the government would have to take my mother and isolate her, which would have been a death sentence. The doctor suggested penicillin, which was relatively new, and my grandmother begged him to stall notifying the government until they could get it. The doctor gave them only a few hours to get the penicillin. They discovered Karbala had it, and Adai drove there in harsh conditions and back with the penicillin to cure my mother.

As he grew older, he came less and less to guard my aunt and grandmother. In his place, his cousin Ahmed took over. As Ahmed grew older, his sons used to protect us. Unlike the older generation, they were unreliable, and ethics slowly disappeared. My aunt's husband, Louis Apikian, had bought my aunt a Peugeot car. She drove it for a few months and traveled to Europe in the summer. Buying a car like this during

Markarian

the Saddam era was difficult and considered a substantial and extravagant novelty. During her time away, she received a call telling her that Ahmed's son had gotten drunk, taken the car, hit six vehicles, and demolished a government wall. Ahmed's son was considered part of the family. My aunt paid for all the damage and a lawyer to get his son out of jail.

The car stayed parked on the dam, with parts disappearing, although the engine was still operative. Regarding people who worked for us, it wasn't debatable whether we would stand by them; it was automatic, an expectation. One day, somebody told my Uncle Louis that he could import a car's body, and since he had the engine, he could assemble a new vehicle. At the peak of the Lebanese civil war, Uncle Louis went to Lebanon and bought a car. When he exported it to Baghdad, the customs seized it since it was a whole car. Since the customs confiscated it, they will sell it at auction. When the car's body came up for auction, a friend of my uncle told the story to the people around, and they refused to bid against my uncle. The auctioneer declared that the car had to reach a specific price to sell. My uncle agreed to buy the vehicle at whatever cost, and by combining the old engine with the new car's body, a new car was ready for my aunt. Unfortunately, the paperwork had gotten lost, which was another obstacle to driving the vehicle. My aunt had an almost new car but sold it seven years later, as it gave her so much grief. It always made me chuckle whenever you took the car to the mechanic, and he returned it with a bag of "extra screws" that came out and were no longer needed when he took it apart.

Mahmood and I

The guards were all related. Adai and Abu Jassim were brothers and cousins to Mahmood and Ahmed, who were also brothers. Mahmood, my mother's guard, taught me how to ride a bicycle. He persuaded my mother to buy me a donkey, and how he drank tea astonished me—he always had one "estekan," a small tea glass with five teaspoons of sugar added to a concentrated tea! Every afternoon, I would rush to go outside to hear his storytelling time about his tribe. He used to say that a thief today has no honor since he steals from anyone, especially those in need, and causes hurt.

One of my favorite stories I used to ask Mahmood to tell me was about his grandmother. Occasionally, in the olden days, his tribe would venture into the city and steal. They would comb through all the districts and then meet on the outskirts. There, they would meet the women of the tribe. The women set up tents and prepared food and entertainment for their tired men, "Chalgi," better known as Iraqi folk music. The thieves would come and visit his grandmother first. She was the tribe's matriarch, and they would display in front of her what they had stolen. She would pick up what she fancied, and they would keep the rest. I loved hearing about her, mainly in how he talked about her. She filled him with pride and awe. The entire tribe held her in high regard and feared his grandmother; she was highly esteemed. Everyone looked up to her and wanted her approval. For a woman at that time, to have such status was rare.

As he got older, he started to become deaf. I remember my mother would send him shopping once in a while. She asked him to get twenty heads of lettuce, "Khas." He came back with twenty large vinegar bottles, "Khal."

Abu Jassim, Mahmood's cousin and Adai's brother, was Uncle Edmond's guard. Their loyalty lay with us, and we were never left alone, especially at my grandmother's house. One of their relatives would come and take their place on their day off. My family was never left alone or neglected. In time, the guards also started to work in other locations and sometimes rotate amongst themselves.

Abu Jassim was a big, tall man with piercing eyes and a defining mustache that cascaded over his mouth. In every sense, he was a man's man. He also had many adventures. One night, he stayed to guard my grandmother's home, and a thief jumped over the railings from the river. Abu Jassim heard him sneaking behind him and caught him. He beat him up to the extent he petrified him, fear paralyzing him from moving. The authorities came the following day and took the thief away. He decided that the cook, Sulaiman, should appear on the court date and declare he caught the thief since the court date conflicted with Abu Jassim's work schedule.

Sulaiman was a flamboyant character. He was weak-looking and had a wild sense of imagination. The judge asked Sulaiman what took place on that fateful night. Being the man he is, Sulaiman goes into the story of his heroic actions of chasing the thief, catching him, and tying him up. The thief, still black and blue from this ordeal, asked the judge to speak. The judge granted the thief his say. The thief affirmed that he did go to rob the house and was caught, but not by Sulaiman. It would be shameful and degrading to know that a man like Sulaiman, not a big, scary-looking giant, overpowered him.

Abu Jassim's cousin used to work for the American Embassy. On his day off, he asked Abu Jassim to stand in his place to guard the embassy. One common thing among all the guards was that they slept on the ground to hear footsteps. One night, Abu Jassim could feel someone approaching. He pretended he was still asleep. Then he noticed the thief had two guns. He sneaked behind him and stole them. Then, he propositioned the thief. He would let him go on the condition that he would leave one of the guns with him. The thief refused. As their voices grew louder and louder, alarms were triggered, resulting in a disturbance. The police arrested the thief, and Abu Jassim received a medal for his heroism.

On my way to school daily, I used to pass by a roundabout symbolizing the story of "Ali Baba and the Forty Thieves." A gigantic statue filled the roundabout, depicting when Morgiana burned the thieves by pouring hot oil into their hiding jars. A black figure of Morgiana stood on top and poured the oil from a big jug she was holding onto the black and green jars. The statue made me think, *You will never catch the real thieves; I grew up with them,* with a big grin on my face.

# Chapter 9

## Food and Traditions

Food is essential in our culture, and the different seasons dictate the availability of the products. Because of the numerous settlements of Armenian people in other countries (Armenia, Iran, India, and Iraq), I have realized that our cuisine seems to adopt the national cuisines but adds a twist to them. Iranian cuisine uses saffron, and Indian cuisine uses curry. Both of those herbs feature in our cooking. The essential thing in our food is the herbs we use: saffron, imported from Iran, and our "buharat," a concoction the family made up through each generation. Tweaking it is paramount. Name Days and holy days were essential days on the calendar. Food is a central theme of their celebrations.

To give you a chance to have an authentic experience of our food, which is so important to us, I have provided some recipes below as part of closing this book. Rather than try to include every recipe important to our culture, I have shared only our favorite family recipes. I hope you also find a love for these dishes and understand a bit more of our extraordinary culture from them.

## Here is the recipe for Minas buharat©, based on proportions:

*¼ cloves, ¼ cinnamon, ¼ allspice, ¼ pepper, ¼ nutmeg, ¼ dried rose petals, ½ - ¾ cardamom. It would make it taste better if you could add the aroma of Shorja (vendors sell herbs in the Shorja district in Baghdad).*

## Ama Zabel's Lamb©:

"Ama Zabel's Lamb" has always been a treat. A leg of lamb is the main ingredient. However, we found that the quality of lamb in Iraq is unavailable in the West as there is little fat, so we sometimes substitute beef.

*Ingredients: 1 leg of lamb, ten garlic cloves, butter, and one tablespoon of tomato paste. Herbs (1 tsp buharat, 1 tsp cloves, 1 tsp cinnamon, 1 tsp cardamom, 1 tsp salt), one big cup red wine vinegar). Also needed: 3 cups of mushrooms, ½ cup of vinegar, and 1 cup of water).*

*Clean the leg of the lamb of fat, making small incisions to bury the garlic cloves into the leg of the lamb, and fry it in the butter by constantly tossing it. Once fried, remove excess butter from the pan and add the tomato paste, buharat, cloves, cinnamon, salt, water,* and vinegar. Cook on low heat for an hour. Make sure the water is not saturated.

Meanwhile, fry the mushrooms. After an hour, add the mushrooms, vinegar, and water to the pan. Fry the mushrooms until tender. Do not forget to ensure the water is not saturated. Serve with red rice.

## Minas's Family Roast©:

One leg of lamb, potatoes, 125g Butter, ½ tsp saffron, 1 tbsp buharat, 1 tsp Salt, four teacups of water, and 1 Turkish coffee cup of rosewater.

Clean the leg of the lamb, remove the fat, and fry. Fry cubed potatoes and put them to the side. Throw the excess butter out and add 125g of butter, saffron, buharat, salt, water, and rosewater. Simmer for two hours on low heat, checking that the water has not evaporated; add more water if it has. Serve with basmati rice with saffron added to it to make it look yellow.

Several of my friends have asked for that recipe, as we cooked it whenever they visited us, and they all felt nostalgic.

## Dejaj Mai Narenj (Chicken in Seville Orange Juice):

One chicken, butter, and potatoes.

Sauce: ½ tsp buharat, ¼ saffron, 2 tsp salt, roux (flour and butter), juice of 1–2 Seville oranges. If not available, you can use lemons and 1 pt of water.

Wash the chicken, rub butter all over it, and bake. Fry the potatoes and put them aside. Put 200g of butter and melt it; add one to two heaped tbsp of flour blend and add the sauce. Then add the chicken and potatoes. Simmer on low heat for an hour.

**Fish in Curry:**

Usually, fried fish is a dish during Easter, but sometimes, the recipe below is an alternative.

One fillet of fish, 400g butter, 1 tsp salt, ½ tsp dried lime (powder), 1 tsp curry powder, ½ tube tomato paste, one bunch parsley, one whole onion, four cloves of garlic, two large tomatoes, 1 cup of vinegar.

Rub salt over the fish, put butter over it, and grill in the oven. Put the fish in milk to get the fishy smell, rest for half an hour, add butter, and cook. Drain the water that has surfaced and add the mixed sauce (fried onion, four cloves of garlic, then add 1 tsp Salt, ½ tsp dried lime (powder), 1 tsp curry powder, ½ tube tomato paste, one bunch parsley, 1 cup of vinegar, and two large tomatoes. The tomatoes are cut into rings and are used to garnish on top of the dish with a bit of parsley.

# Conclusion

Every one of us has a story to tell. Each family has a tale to tell. I am no different. I wanted to capture the struggles and accomplishments of my family. Everyone leaves a legacy, good or bad, poor or rich, and I wanted to focus on that. Times have changed from those of my ancestors, grandparents, and parents, and I wanted to share a glimpse into their time and document it.

I have learned that applying integrity, loyalty, and honesty into your life is very difficult and easier said than done since diversions, pressures, and self-interest come in the way, but ultimately, those qualities will give you value amongst humanity. You choose your friends, so choose wisely. Family should not be entitled just because you share their DNA; DNA gives them no right to disrespect or take advantage of you.

I hope you have enjoyed my book. If I enlightened you, made you reflect, or even smile, I would have accomplished my goal of sharing this information.

# About the Author

Zagheek Markarian lives in Toronto, Canada, but spent a part of her youth as an Armenian living in Iraq. She grew up in Europe, mainly in London, U.K., and spent a stint in the U.A.E. She works in education and documents historical events. She holds pride in her family, heritage, and cultural history. With this background and to offer her daughters a historical account of their heritage, she was inspired to write this book.

Printed in the USA
CPSIA information can be obtained
at www.ICGtesting.com
LVHW091935140724
785345LV00001B/176

9 781039 193635